EVERYONE LOVES ME

The Art of Creating Authentic Friends and Lasting Love

By
Robert Hayes

Everyone Loves Me

Get 3 FREE Tools That Change Everything

I appreciate you!!!

Thank you for reading Everyone Loves Me. These three free companion tools are deeply personal, born from my own healing, research, and hard-won lessons. They're the most powerful, practical resources I've ever created. If the book spoke to you, these will take you even deeper.

Click the link or scan the QR code below. Then just enter your email. I'll send you immediate access to all three free programs, along with additional resources as I continue to write and research solutions for you.

Three Free Tools. One New You

Drop the Mask. Be Seen. Be Loved. What kind of thinker are you? Take the quiz. Meet your mind. Then start thinking like someone who trusts themselves and lives without second-guessing every move.

Boost Confidence and Become Someone Nobody Forgets.
Confidence isn't a mystery, it's a habit. Build it one small step at a time. From overthinking and awkward to unforgettable and magnetic in just one powerful week.

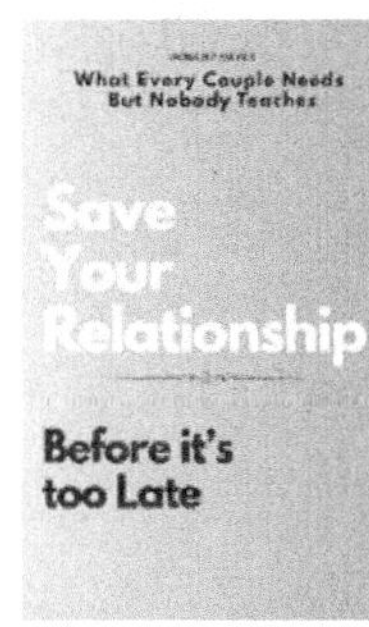

What Every Couple Needs But Nobody Teaches.
The repair manual you never got. Fix what's fading. Rebuild what matters. Real tools to reconnect deeply, before "fine" quietly turns into falling apart.

Don't Stop Here, Let's Go Deeper

Click the Link or Scan the QR Code for FREE Access

Visit: www.roberthayesbooks.com/loves/

A Personal Favor from Robert Hayes

I need your help...

If Everyone Loves Me meant something to you, if it helped you feel seen, stronger, or a little more loved, I'd be deeply grateful if you'd take 60 seconds to leave a great review on Amazon.

This book is my life's mission. Your review isn't just feedback, it's a lifeline.

Your words can encourage someone else to begin their healing, to feel hope, to believe change is possible.

This message spreads to one person at a time, not through ads, but through readers like you.

Thank you for reading. Thank you for being part of this.

Scan this QR Code to Leave a Review

Also, if you'd like to stay in the loop about upcoming books and updates, follow me on Instagram at **@robert_h_author**

or scan the QR Code:

@ROBERT_H_AUTHOR_

A Video That Might Change Your Life

Reading Everyone Loves Me is a powerful awakening.

But what if you could put it into action, faster, clearer, with more impact?

This short video is the Quick Start many of my most successful clients have used to transform everything.

It's not for everyone. But if you're serious about change, and want momentum, not just insight, this is where things really start moving.

No pressure. No expectations. Just one video that might flip the switch.

Watch now. The next version of you is waiting.

Visit: www.roberthayesbooks.com/loves/video

Or scan the QR Code below.

CONTENTS

Introduction

Have you ever walked into a room and felt invisible? Have you ever struggled with the fear that no matter what you do, it will never be enough? Maybe you've replayed conversations in your mind, obsessing over what you should have said, or worse, what people think of you. If you've ever wrestled with self-doubt, felt the sting of loneliness, or wondered why relationships seem so hard, you're in the right place.

This book is not about becoming "perfect" or faking confidence. It's about becoming the most powerful version of yourself. The one that already exists beneath self-doubt, toxic thinking, and old stories that no longer serve you.

What This Book Will Help You Do

In the following chapters, you'll discover a step-by-step journey to breaking free from insecurity, forming deeper relationships, and stepping into a life of confidence and connection. Each chapter builds on the last, giving you the tools to:

- Accept yourself fully (even the parts you think are "flaws").
- Recognize toxic behaviors that push people away and replace them with ones that draw others in.

- Rewrite the negative stories in your head and build unshakable confidence.
- Shift your focus outward learning how to make others feel seen and appreciated.
- Develop the kind of courage that creates meaningful, lasting relationships.

This is not a book about pretending to be someone you're not. It's about stripping away the insecurities, self-sabotage, and doubts that have held you back so you can finally show up as the person you were meant to be.

I know what it's like to feel stuck. To battle thoughts that tell you you're not good enough, or that you'll never truly belong. That's why I've spent my life studying relationships, self-growth, and the way our minds shape our reality.

I'm Robert Hayes, and my work focuses on cognitive behavioral psychology and personal transformation. Over the years, I've worked with countless individuals to help them break free from limiting beliefs and rediscover their potential. This book isn't about abstract theories. It's a practical guide rooted in proven methods and real-world insights. Whether you're here because you struggle with self-confidence, want stronger relationships, or simply feel stuck in old patterns, I want you to know you're not alone and change is possible.

If you're tired of second-guessing yourself, feeling stuck in old patterns, or craving deeper connections but don't know where to start, this book will give you the answers.

1

Being Okay with Not Being Okay

A friend once shared a story that resonated deeply with me. She was preparing for a presentation, nerves gnawing at her confidence. As she stood in front of the mirror, she noticed her hands trembling. Instead of criticizing herself for being anxious, she paused, took a deep breath, and whispered, "It's okay to be nervous. It's okay to be me." This simple act of acceptance transformed her experience. She still felt nervous, but she also felt empowered. That day, she realized something profound: it's perfectly okay not to have it all together.

You see, life isn't about achieving perfection; it's about embracing our imperfections and finding strength in vulnerability. In our pursuit of self-improvement, we often overlook the beauty hidden within our flaws. Yet, these imperfections are not failures; they are the unique traits that make us human and relatable. As you navigate your own path, consider this: "nobody is perfect, and striving for perfection" can alienate you from your authentic self (Poised & Proper, n.d.). It's the raw, unfiltered version of you that people connect with. The one who doesn't hide behind a facade.

The Beauty of Being Flawed

Why Flaws Make You Unique: When you look in the mirror, what do you see? Perhaps you notice the things you wish were different. The crooked smile, the shy demeanor, or the tendency to overthink. But what if these perceived flaws are not weaknesses but rather the very things that make you special? Embrace them. They are the brushstrokes of your unique canvas.

Throughout life, we encounter individuals who seem effortlessly perfect, yet it is those who reveal their true selves, imperfections, and all, who leave a lasting impression. It is through vulnerability that we find connection, and through acceptance that we cultivate authentic relationships. People connect more deeply with those who are authentic rather than those who seem flawless.

Consider the story of Noah, a man who once believed his shyness held him back. For years, he avoided social gatherings, convinced his quiet nature made him uninteresting. One day, he decided to attend a community event, determined to step outside his comfort zone. Instead of pretending to be outgoing, he embraced his introspective nature. To his surprise, he found that others were drawn to his thoughtful demeanor. Conversations flowed effortlessly, and friendships blossomed. Noah's greatest strength emerged not by masking his shyness, but by embracing it as a valuable trait.

In a world that often prioritizes superficial perfection, finding the courage to embrace your imperfections is a radical act of self-love. It takes bravery to stand in the truth of who you are, flaws and all. This self-acceptance is the first step toward building deeper connections. When you allow yourself to be seen, truly seen, you create a space where others feel safe to do the same. Vulnerability is contagious; when you admit your imperfections, you open the door for others to share theirs.

The Courage to Embrace Imperfection: Begin by considering one trait you perceive as a flaw. Write it down. Now, reframe it as something that makes you unique. For instance, if you consider yourself overly cautious, perhaps you are, in fact, deeply thoughtful and observant. This exercise shifts your perspective, allowing you to view yourself through a lens of compassion.

Acknowledge that nobody has it all figured out. We all carry scars, fears, and insecurities. But it is in these very imperfections that our humanity shines through. Embracing them is not only liberating but also transformative. It means acknowledging that you are a work in progress, and that's perfectly okay. When you embrace your flaws, you send a message to the world: you are enough, just as you are. This courage to stand authentically inspires those around you to do the same.

In your journey toward self-love and acceptance, remember that perfection is an illusion. It is your imperfections, your quirks, and your vulnerabilities that create the tapestry of your life. They are not to be hidden but celebrated. Every flaw tells a story, and every story weaves the fabric of your existence. So, take a moment to appreciate the beauty of being flawed, for it is within these imperfections that your true strength lies.

Emotions Are Messy And That's Okay

Life is a tapestry of emotions, each thread weaving its own story. This emotional spectrum, ranging from joy to sorrow, is a natural part of being human. Yet, society often pressures us to categorize these feelings into neat boxes labeled "good" or "bad." This dichotomy can lead to a cycle of self-criticism and shame. Emotions, however, are not to be judged but to be experienced. They ebb and flow, much like waves crashing upon the shore, each one different from the last. When you recognize this, you allow yourself the freedom to feel without restraint.

To foster emotional balance, try not to label your emotions. Instead, let them pass through you like visitors, each with a message to convey. Journaling can be a powerful tool here. Pouring your thoughts onto paper without judgment creates space for clarity. It's a practice that allows you to step back, observe, and understand what you're truly feeling. In doing so, you cultivate a sense of acceptance and peace.

Emotional honesty is the cornerstone of authentic relationships. Sharing your struggles with trusted individuals can weave a bond stronger than any facade of perfection. It requires courage to say, "I feel [emotion] because of [reason], and that's okay." This simple statement acknowledges your emotions and allows others to see your true self. Emotional honesty is a skill, that demands practice and patience. When you open up about your feelings, you invite others to do the same, creating a space of mutual understanding and empathy.

Consider the research presented in Psychology Today, which highlights how emotional honesty enriches relationships by fostering intimacy and trust. By embracing the full range of your emotions, you not only deepen your connections but also strengthen your sense of self.

Take, for instance, the case of a corporate executive who appeared to have it all. On the surface, he radiated confidence and success. Yet, beneath this polished exterior, he grappled with feelings of inadequacy and fear. It wasn't until he began to share his inner struggles with a mentor that he found relief. In revealing his vulnerabilities, he discovered a newfound strength. His mentor's response was not one of judgment but of understanding and support. This interaction transformed his perspective, teaching him the strength of vulnerability and the power of emotional honesty. By allowing himself to be seen, he forged a deeper connection, not only with his mentor but with himself.

This chapter sets the stage for what is to come, laying the groundwork for exploring vulnerability more deeply in later chapters. As you continue reading, remember that embracing your emotions is an act of courage. It is the first step toward cultivating the vulnerability and courage needed to deepen your relationships, as we will explore further in Chapter 10.

Find Strength in the Struggle

Struggles and challenges are often seen as burdens to bear, yet they hold a remarkable power to transform and redefine us. Each obstacle we face is a chance to grow, to become more resilient, and to learn invaluable lessons that shape who we are. Consider the experience of a young teacher, someone who had to navigate the complexities of a demanding profession while grappling with self-doubt. Initially, every setback felt like a confirmation of inadequacy. But over time, she began to view these struggles as opportunities.

Every difficult lesson plan, and every challenging student, taught her patience, empathy, and creativity. She learned to adapt, to find solutions where none seemed possible, and in doing so, she discovered a strength she never knew she had. This transformation did not occur overnight. It was a gradual unfolding that took place as she allowed herself to learn from each challenge.

Brené Brown, a leading researcher on vulnerability, emphasizes that embracing our struggles with openness and curiosity can lead to profound personal growth. In understanding our vulnerabilities, we gain the courage to face life's uncertainties with a renewed sense of purpose and strength.

Challenging negative thoughts is a crucial step in finding strength within the struggle. Often, our minds are clouded by cognitive distortions, thought patterns that skew our perception, and reinforce limiting beliefs. These distortions can range from black-and-white thinking, where we see situations in extremes, to overgeneralization, where a single failure becomes a perceived pattern of incompetence. For instance, you might tell yourself, "I failed once, so I'll always fail." Such thoughts are not only inaccurate but also self-defeating.

Cognitive Behavior Therapy (CBT) offers practical techniques to identify and reframe these distortions. By recognizing these patterns, you can begin to question their validity and replace them with constructive beliefs. For example, instead of clinging to the belief that a single failure defines you, consider reframing it as, "I'm learning, and mistakes help me grow." This shift in thinking opens the door to self-compassion and resilience, allowing you to embrace challenges as opportunities rather than threats.

Exercise: Take a moment to reflect on a past challenge. Write down what you learned from it and how it has contributed to your growth. This exercise connects to the theme of rewriting stories, which we will explore in depth in Chapter 7. By acknowledging the lessons hidden within hardship, you take the first step in transforming adversity into a catalyst for personal evolution. This practice not only changes how you view your past but also empowers you to approach future challenges with a mindset of growth and possibility. Embracing the struggle, with all its messiness and uncertainty, is not about denying the difficulties you face. It's about choosing to see beyond them, to recognize the potential for growth and strength that lies within each experience. This perspective fosters resilience, allowing you to navigate life's complexities with grace and determination.

As we continue, keep in mind the power of reframing your thoughts. This skill will be revisited extensively in Chapter 7, where we will delve deeper into the process of rewriting the narratives that shape our lives.

Be Kind to the Person You See in the Mirror

The journey to self-compassion begins with the person staring back at you in the mirror. It is about offering yourself "the same kindness and understanding that you would offer a dear friend" (LR Wellness, n.d.). This act of self-compassion is particularly vital during moments of failure or imperfection when the voice of self-criticism tends to be the loudest. Instead of engaging in harsh self-talk, try replacing those thoughts with affirmations such as, "It's okay to make mistakes; I'm still learning." Such affirmations serve as gentle reminders that imperfection is a universal experience, and that growth often originates from setbacks.

According to Kristin Neff, a pioneering researcher in this field, "self-compassion involves being warm and understanding toward ourselves when we suffer, fail, or feel inadequate, rather than ignoring our pain or flagellating ourselves with self-criticism." Her research indicates that self-compassion is linked "to greater emotional resilience, reduced levels of anxiety and depression," and overall well-being (Serenities Path, n.d.). By treating ourselves with kindness, we foster an internal environment where growth can flourish.

Consider the story of a college student who, after failing a crucial exam, was consumed by self-doubt. Initially, she berated herself, convinced that this failure defined her academic capabilities. However, after encountering Neff's work, she decided to approach herself with compassion. She began to view the failure not as a reflection of her worth but as an opportunity to learn and improve. By replacing her inner critic with a voice of support, she rebuilt her confidence and approached her studies with renewed focus and determination. This shift in mindset not only improved her grades but also enhanced her overall sense of self-worth. Her story exemplifies how self-compassion can transform self-doubt into self-assurance, allowing us to see setbacks as steppingstones rather than stumbling blocks.

Practicing self-kindness daily can lay the groundwork for a healthier self-image. Simple exercises can ease you into this habit. One effective method is writing a supportive letter to yourself as if you were comforting a close friend. In this letter, acknowledge your struggles and offer words of encouragement. By externalizing your thoughts, you can gain perspective and cultivate a nurturing inner dialogue. Another daily practice is to pause and acknowledge small victories, no matter how trivial they may seem. Celebrating these moments reinforces a positive self-view and counteracts negativity.

Self-compassion not only nurtures personal growth but also strengthens the emotional foundation necessary for building deeper relationships. When you show kindness to yourself, you become more capable of extending that same kindness to others. This principle will be revisited in Chapter 8, where the interplay between self-compassion and meaningful connections will be explored in greater depth.

Understanding and practicing self-compassion is an ongoing process, one that evolves as you continue to learn and grow. It requires patience and persistence, but the rewards are profound, enhanced resilience, greater self-acceptance, and the ability to face life's challenges with confidence and courage. As you cultivate this practice, remember that self-compassion is not about erasing imperfections but about embracing them as integral parts of your humanity. It is about recognizing that you are deserving of love and kindness, just as you are.

Let Go of Perfect, and Embrace the Real

In a world that often equates success with flawlessness, the pursuit of perfection can become an all-consuming endeavor. Perfectionism, though seemingly noble, often stems from a fear of judgment rather than a genuine desire to improve. This fear can create a cycle of relentless self-criticism and anxiety, leaving us feeling disconnected from ourselves and those around us. We set impossible standards, not only for ourselves but for our relationships, causing stress and missed opportunities for genuine connection.

In the quest for an unattainable ideal, we often overlook the beauty of authenticity. Our relationships can suffer as we impose unrealistic expectations on others, expecting them to conform to an idealized version of themselves. This rigidity stifles growth and prevents us from experiencing the joy that comes with embracing the real.

Let me tell you about Emma, a graphic designer who once believed that her work and her life had to be perfect to be valuable. She spent countless hours tweaking every detail of her projects, often missing deadlines and feeling perpetually dissatisfied. Her personal relationships mirrored this pattern, as she expected others to meet her exacting standards. It wasn't until she experienced burnout that Emma began to question her relentless pursuit.

To find balance, she decided to let go of her need for perfection. Instead of striving for flawlessness, she focused on progress, allowing herself to make mistakes and learn from them. Emma discovered that by releasing her unrealistic expectations, she found more joy in her work and deeper connections with those around her. Her creativity flourished, and her relationships became more meaningful. This shift not only transformed her professional life but also enriched her personal interactions, as she learned to appreciate the imperfections that make each of us unique.

To embrace progress over perfection, consider setting achievable expectations for yourself. The SMART goals framework Specific, Measurable, Achievable, Relevant, and Time-bound which can be an effective tool. By creating goals that are realistic and attainable, you allow yourself the space to grow without the pressure of perfection. This approach encourages you to celebrate small victories, fostering a sense of accomplishment and motivation.

As you set these goals, take a moment to reflect on the question: "What would happen if I let go of needing to be perfect?" This reflection invites you to explore the possibilities that come with embracing authenticity. It challenges you to consider how releasing the burden of perfection might open doors to new experiences and deeper connections. It is in this space of acceptance that true growth occurs.

Embracing the real requires courage, yet it offers a freedom that perfectionism cannot. When you let go of the need for perfection, you create room for the genuine, the flawed, and the beautiful aspects of life. You allow yourself to be present, to engage fully with the world around you, and to form connections based on authenticity rather than illusion.

This transition from perfectionism to authenticity is not about lowering standards or settling for less. It is about recognizing that life's richness lies not in the flawless execution of tasks but in the messy, unpredictable, and wonderful experiences that make us human. It is about understanding "that perfection is an illusion, and that true fulfillment comes from embracing" the real (Inoa Juice, n.d.).

As you move forward, remember that the path to self-acceptance is not a race. It is a continuous process of learning and growth, one that invites you to let go of perfection and embrace the real. This chapter invites you to explore the freedom and joy that come with authenticity. By choosing to be real, you open yourself to a world of possibilities, where imperfection is celebrated, and authenticity is valued. In this space, you find the courage to be yourself, to connect deeply with others, and to live a life that is truly your own.

2

How to Make Everyone Hate You

Have you ever felt like people are quietly pulling away from you, but you're not sure why? Sometimes, it's not what we say, but the habits we bring into our relationships that push others away. These behaviors often go unnoticed, slowly eroding trust and connection over time.

This chapter isn't about blame, it's about awareness. We all have blind spots, patterns that keep us stuck in cycles of frustration and loneliness. The goal here is to recognize them, not to dwell in guilt, but to understand what might be holding you back. Because once you see the problem clearly, you can finally do something about it.

1. Being Chronically Negative

Consider your daily interactions. How often do you find yourself complaining about the trivialities of life? Maybe you blame external circumstances for your internal dissatisfaction. This kind of communication style, centered around negativity, can push people away. Friends and colleagues may start to withdraw, tired of the constant stream of complaints and blame that never seems to abate. Relationships that once felt vibrant and nurturing begin to crumble under the weight of relentless pessimism.

An example is a colleague who, despite his competence, finds himself increasingly isolated at work. Every conversation turns into a lament about management, clients, or the state of the world. At first, people listen, offering sympathy. But over time, they grow weary. Negativity, when constant, becomes draining. Eventually, his peers stop including him in discussions, leaving him on the periphery. The irony? His negativity, intended as a call for change, only solidifies his isolation.

Few people actively seek out negativity. Instead, they gravitate toward those who uplift, encourage, and bring some sense of optimism to a conversation. Even when challenges arise, how you express yourself determines whether others want to engage with you or distance themselves. Constant negativity whether it's complaining, criticizing, or always expecting the worst creates an environment that repels others.

Over time, this habit can alter the way people perceive you. You may find that friends stop inviting you out, coworkers avoid unnecessary conversations, and even those closest to you begin limiting their interactions. Not because they don't care, but because being around you starts to feel like emotional labor.

The result? A vicious cycle where negativity breeds isolation, and isolation fuels even more negativity.

2. Being Self-Centered

Imagine sitting at a dinner table, surrounded by friends, yet feeling a subtle disconnect. As the conversation unfolds, you find yourself steering it back to your achievements, your stories, and your needs. This is the essence of a self-centered mindset, where the focus remains on oneself, often leaving others feeling unseen and undervalued.

When conversations become a monologue rather than a dialogue, relationships start to fray. The more someone talks about themselves, the less room there is for others to contribute. Over time, this dynamic can create resentment, even if unintentional. Friends and colleagues may begin to feel like mere spectators in your life rather than valued participants in a meaningful exchange.

A lack of reciprocity in conversations can create an emotional distance that is hard to repair. Perhaps you've experienced this imbalance. Eager to share something important, only to have the other person pivot the conversation back to themselves. It feels dismissive as if your thoughts and feelings are secondary. The same thing happens when you become the one doing it. Even when unintentional, prioritizing your own voice over others sends a message: their experiences, struggles, and victories don't matter as much.

Over time, this behavior erodes trust. People begin to withdraw, not because they don't care, but because they don't feel valued. Relationships that were once filled with warmth and mutual appreciation can begin to feel transactional, where interactions serve one person's needs more than the other's.

Eventually, self-centeredness leads to isolation. The more conversations become one-sided; the fewer people stick around to have them.

3. Being Unreliable

Trust is the cornerstone of any meaningful relationship, yet it is fragile and easily eroded by inconsistency and broken promises. Imagine a friend who repeatedly cancels plans at the last minute or a colleague who misses deadlines without warning. Over time, these patterns of unreliability create a landscape of disappointment and resentment. Every missed commitment chips away at the foundation of trust, leaving behind a sense of betrayal and insecurity.

Trust, once lost, is incredibly difficult to regain, much like trying to piece together a shattered vase. It requires a conscious effort to rebuild what was once carelessly disregarded. The emotional toll of unreliability extends beyond the immediate consequences. It fosters a climate of uncertainty where others feel they cannot rely on you. This uncertainty breeds frustration and weakens bonds, making it challenging to establish genuine connections.

A partner who cannot trust your word will eventually grow weary of excuses, and a friend who feels let down may choose to distance themselves.

The impact of unreliability is profound, affecting not only personal relationships but professional ones as well. Coworkers may hesitate to collaborate with someone who consistently misses deadlines, while social circles may exclude those who fail to show up when it matters. Over time, the reputation of being unreliable can become a defining trait, pushing people further away and making it harder to rebuild trust.

4. Criticizing Constantly

In the tapestry of human interaction, criticism can unravel even the strongest threads. It's a force that slowly erodes trust and intimacy, leaving behind defensiveness and distance. Constant judgment, whether it's delivered as unsolicited advice or incessant fault-finding, creates an environment where people feel they must always be on guard. This dynamic turns conversations into battlegrounds, where each party is more focused on defending their position than on understanding or connecting with the other.

Picture a friend who, despite their best intentions, habitually points out your flaws, offering advice you never asked for. Over time, you might start avoiding them, not because you don't value their friendship, but because their words make you feel inadequate. The weight of continuous criticism fosters self-doubt, making people question their worth in relationships.

Criticism, especially when relentless, drives a wedge between individuals. It fosters a defensive stance, where the criticized person feels compelled to justify their actions or choices, rather than engaging in open dialogue. This defensiveness weakens bonds, transforming what could be a constructive exchange into a cycle of hurt and resentment. Relationships built on such shaky ground often struggle to withstand the test of time.

Consider how a parent who constantly criticizes might inadvertently push their child to rebel or withdraw, not out of spite but as a means of self-preservation. The same pattern applies in friendships and romantic relationships when someone feels they can never measure up and they begin to distance themselves. Over time, this creates an emotional chasm, replacing connection with resentment and leaving relationships fragile and strained.

5. Gossiping

Gossip, an alluring yet destructive force, can unravel "the fabric of trust that holds relationships together" (Sanctuary Foundation, n.d.). At first glance, gossip might seem harmless, a casual exchange of news or an attempt to bond over shared information. Yet beneath its surface lies a toxic undercurrent that erodes connections and breed's distrust. When you spread rumors, you betray the confidence others place in you, creating rifts that can shatter friendships.

Imagine a once-close circle of friends, torn apart by whispers and half-truths. What began as idle chatter turns into a tangled web of deceit, leaving hurt and betrayal in its wake. The psychological appeal of gossip lies in its ability to make us feel included or informed, yet it often comes at the expense of loyalty and integrity.

Gossip fosters a culture of mistrust, where individuals question the sincerity of their relationships. If someone is willing to talk about others behind their backs, what's stopping them from doing the same to you? The more someone engages in gossip, the more people begin to keep their distance, fearing they may become the next target. Over time, this damages relationships, creating an environment of suspicion rather than genuine connection.

Friendships built on trust can quickly dissolve when gossip becomes a habit. Even those who once confided in you may withdraw, unsure if their words will remain private. A reputation for gossiping can be difficult to shake, as people become wary of opening up. Instead of fostering deeper bonds, gossip ultimately isolates, leaving behind a trail of broken relationships and missed opportunities for true connection.

6. Being Emotionally Unavailable

Imagine a world where everyone around you feels like a distant figure, not because they are far away, but because you've built an emotional wall. Emotional detachment, often a defense mechanism, can create vast chasms in relationships. It's the subtle art of withholding vulnerability, of dismissing not only your own emotions but those of others.

Picture this: a friend sharing a heartfelt story, hoping for empathy, but instead, you offer a nod and change the subject. Over time, this avoidance of vulnerability and dismissal of emotions creates a barrier, leaving others feeling unseen and unheard. Conversations begin to feel hollow, interactions become surface-level, and meaningful connections fade into the background.

This detachment doesn't just affect others; it impacts you as well. The habit of shutting down emotions or refusing to engage with the emotional needs of others fosters an environment of isolation. People may still be physically present in your life, but emotionally, the distance grows. Over time, trust erodes, and relationships shift from deep and meaningful to transactional and empty.

Emotional unavailability can also create frustration in those closest to you. Loved ones may feel as though they are constantly reaching out, only to be met with coldness or indifference. Eventually, they stop trying. The long-term effects can be profound, as people who once felt safe with you begin to look elsewhere for emotional support. Without emotional engagement, relationships weaken, leaving both parties disconnected and unfulfilled.

7. Being Manipulative

Manipulative behaviors can insidiously creep into relationships, eroding trust and respect. These tactics such as guilt-tripping, gaslighting, and exploitation slowly chip away at the foundation of healthy connections. Guilt-tripping makes someone feel responsible for your emotions or actions, subtly shifting the blame onto them. Gaslighting is even more insidious, causing someone to doubt their own perceptions and sanity. Exploitation takes advantage of someone's vulnerability for personal gain, turning trust into a tool for control.

At first, manipulation may appear to strengthen a relationship by ensuring compliance or control, but over time, it corrodes respect. When people feel manipulated, they begin to question whether their emotions and decisions are truly their own. Relationships built on manipulation breed resentment, fear, and an unspoken power imbalance that makes genuine trust impossible.

People manipulate for different reasons, often as a defense mechanism. Fear of rejection, insecurity, or a need for control can drive someone to use manipulation as a way to maintain relationships on their own terms. However, what begins as a means of self-protection ultimately results in loneliness. Over time, those on the receiving end grow weary of feeling controlled, deceived, or guilted into actions they wouldn't otherwise choose. Eventually, they pull away. What once felt like influence or connection turns into a cycle of distrust and emotional distance.

8. Never Admitting Fault

Imagine a scenario where a disagreement occurs, and instead of owning up to your role, you deflect blame. Perhaps you insist, "It's not my fault" or "You misunderstood me," shifting the focus away from your actions. This habit of refusing accountability might feel like self-preservation, a way to protect your ego and avoid discomfort. But in reality, it weakens the foundation of trust in your relationships.

When we deny responsibility, we sow seeds of resentment and distrust. Over time, these seeds grow into barriers that make authentic connections nearly impossible. Those around you start to see you as someone who refuses to acknowledge mistakes or make amends, which can leave them feeling disillusioned, frustrated, and unappreciated.

This avoidance also creates emotional distance. Friends, family members, and colleagues may begin to question your integrity and reliability. They might stop confiding in you, feeling that any attempt at meaningful dialogue will be met with defensiveness rather than openness. As relationships deteriorate, the damage can extend beyond the immediate moment. People may hesitate to depend on you in the future, assuming that any conflict will be met with excuses rather than accountability.

At its core, refusing to admit fault is an isolating behavior. The more someone avoids responsibility, the harder it becomes to maintain deep, trusting relationships. Without accountability, bonds slowly break down, leaving behind fractured connections that are difficult to repair.

9. Being Jealous or Envious

Envy creeps into friendships like a silent specter, poisoning the well of trust and camaraderie. You might find yourself eyeing a friend's success with resentment, your mind whispering, "Why not me?" This insidious feeling can lead to competitiveness, passive-aggressive remarks, or even a subtle desire to see others fail just to make yourself feel better.

Picture a friend celebrating a promotion. Instead of sharing in their joy, envy might prompt you to downplay their success or highlight your own struggles, creating an emotional chasm. What could have been a moment of celebration turns into an internal battle of comparison and resentment. You might smile and say congratulations, but deep down, there's a sting of bitterness, a feeling that their win somehow diminishes you.

Jealousy breeds distance. It makes people withdraw, hesitate to share their wins, or even feel the need to compete rather than connect. Over time, relationships become strained, laced with unspoken tension. Trust is slowly eroded, as envy turns admiration into quiet hostility. The more it festers, the harder it becomes to maintain healthy friendships.

Even when unspoken, jealousy is felt. It shows up in subtle ways like less enthusiasm when a friend shares good news, avoiding certain topics, or downplaying someone's success in conversation. Instead of strengthening bonds, it creates emotional walls. Friendships become transactional rather than genuine, and instead of cheering each other on, people find themselves keeping score.

At its core, jealousy is isolating. It shifts the focus from mutual connection to silent rivalry, creating a wedge between people who could otherwise lift each other up. The irony is that the more envy takes hold, the lonelier a person becomes, unable to fully enjoy the relationships that could bring them fulfillment.

10. Overstepping Boundaries

Imagine standing too close to someone in a conversation, feeling the tension as their discomfort becomes palpable. This is a simple yet vivid example of overstepping boundaries. But boundaries extend beyond physical space. They encompass emotional and mental limits as well. When someone consistently disregards these unspoken lines, whether by pushing too hard for personal details, imposing their needs on others, or failing to respect personal autonomy, it creates friction in relationships.

Overstepping boundaries can take many forms. Some people dominate conversations, offering unsolicited advice or pressing for information that isn't theirs to know. Others expect constant availability, failing to recognize that friendships and relationships require balance. This type of behavior can come across as controlling, intrusive, or even suffocating. While the intent may not always be malicious, the impact can still be damaging.

At first, people might tolerate small boundary violations out of politeness or reluctance to create conflict. But over time, unchecked boundary-crossing erodes trust. It makes others feel like their personal space whether physical, emotional, or mental is being invaded. This often leads to silent resentment, avoidance, or even abrupt distancing from the relationship.

When someone ignores or disrespects boundaries, the natural response is withdrawal. People instinctively protect themselves from those who make them feel uncomfortable, unheard, or manipulated. It creates an undercurrent of unease, making interactions feel forced or tense rather than natural and safe. The more boundaries are ignored, the greater the distance becomes, until what was once a close relationship starts to feel like a burden.

The reality is that relationships thrive on mutual respect. When boundaries are crossed repeatedly, they chip away at that foundation, leaving behind discomfort and strained connections. The hardest part? Those who overstep boundaries often don't realize the damage they're doing until it's too late.

A Hard Truth, A New Beginning

To wrap up this chapter, I want you to take a moment and reflect on what we've just covered. If any of these behaviors resonated with you, don't panic. This isn't about shame or self-blame. It's about awareness. The truth is, we've all fallen into these patterns at some point. Maybe you've caught yourself being overly critical, unreliable, or even emotionally distant. The good news? Recognizing these tendencies is the first step toward change.

This chapter wasn't meant to tear you down, it was meant to hold up a mirror, to challenge you to see yourself with honesty and clarity. Because once you do, you gain the power to rewrite the story.

In the next chapter, we'll continue examining the patterns that sabotage relationships, digging even deeper into two of the most destructive forces that can push people away. Then, as we move forward, we'll shift toward solutions. How to break free from these habits and build the kind of relationships that bring fulfillment and joy.

So, keep going. You've already done the hardest part which is facing the truth. Now, let's move forward together.

3

The Two Core Cancers of Friendship Killers

In the intricate tapestry of human relationships, insecurity often weaves a thread of silent sabotage. It lurks in the shadows of our minds, whispering doubts and fears that can fracture even the strongest bonds. Insecurity is not merely a fleeting feeling; it is a deep-rooted fear of inadequacy, rejection, or failure. It masquerades behind destructive behaviors, eroding self-worth and hindering genuine connections.

Marianne Williamson eloquently captures this sentiment with her observation: "Our deepest fear is not that we are inadequate. Our deepest fear is that we are powerful beyond measure" (Williamson, 1992). This powerful insight suggests that at the heart of insecurity lies not just the fear of failing, but the fear of succeeding and realizing our full potential. As you navigate the complexities of relationships, understanding insecurity's insidious role can illuminate the path to more authentic and fulfilling connections.

1. Insecurity: The Silent Saboteur of Relationships

Insecurity thrives on comparison, sowing seeds of jealousy and envy that can corrode even the most cherished friendships. It's that nagging voice that questions your worth about others, leaving you feeling insufficient and resentful. Imagine discovering that a close friend has embarked on a new relationship, and instead of sharing in their joy, you find yourself making passive-aggressive remarks aimed at undermining their happiness. This behavior stems from insecurity, from a place where your fears of inadequacy overshadow the ability to genuinely celebrate another's success. Such actions not only harm your friend but also deepen the chasm of insecurity within, further isolating you from the warmth of true connection.

Social media has amplified this dynamic in ways never seen before. Platforms designed for connection often become arenas of silent competition where carefully curated highlight reels fuel feelings of inadequacy. You may find yourself scrolling through endless images of friends on vacations, celebrating promotions, or attending gatherings you weren't invited to. Without realizing it, comparison seeps in, leaving a bitter taste of self-doubt. The more we compare, the less we feel valued in our own lives, creating a silent wedge between us and the people we once felt close to.

Chronic negativity is another manifestation of insecurity, pulling you into a vortex of self-pity and despair. This mindset often surfaces as a constant stream of complaints and grievances, a desperate attempt to garner sympathy and validation. However, rather than drawing people closer, it tends to push them away, as they grow weary of the relentless negativity. Imagine a scenario where every conversation turns into a litany of woes, each complaint a thinly veiled plea for reassurance. Over time, friends may begin to distance themselves, unable to shoulder the burden of your unhappiness. This cycle of negativity, fueled by insecurity, not only diminishes your relationships but also perpetuates a sense of isolation and despair.

Consider a workplace scenario: an employee constantly down plays their achievements and worries excessively about how they are perceived by colleagues. They hesitate to speak in meetings, fearing judgment, or become defensive when given constructive feedback. Over time, their insecurity creates tension, making coworkers hesitant to collaborate with them. This distance is not because others dislike them, but because the emotional exhaustion of managing their insecurity becomes too much to bear. Relationships suffer not because of an external betrayal, but because of an internal war that leaves others unsure of how to engage.

Criticism and gossip, too, find their roots in insecurity, serving as misguided attempts to mask perceived shortcomings. By tearing others down, you may temporarily elevate your sense of self-worth, but this fleeting satisfaction comes at a significant cost. It creates an atmosphere of distrust and animosity, where genuine connection becomes increasingly difficult to achieve. Imagine the impact of spreading rumors about a colleague or constantly nitpicking a friend's choices. These actions, driven by insecurity, not only damage others but also corrode your integrity, leaving behind a trail of broken relationships and wounded hearts.

Insecurity can also lead to extreme emotional reactions. For instance, a person who constantly fears abandonment might overreact to a friend canceling plans. They may assume it's a sign of rejection rather than an innocent scheduling conflict, leading to unnecessary arguments and resentment. These patterns push people away and reinforce the very fears insecurity thrives on. The irony of insecurity is that the more we succumb to it, the more we create the conditions we fear most: isolation, rejection, and disconnection.

Psychologists suggest that insecurity often develops early in life, shaped by experiences of criticism, neglect, or comparison. When a child grows up feeling they must earn love through achievement or perfection, they may carry these anxieties into adulthood. This learned behavior leads to an endless cycle of self-doubt and approval-seeking, which can unknowingly strain relationships. Understanding this root cause can help break the cycle and foster healthier self-perceptions and interpersonal dynamics.

2. Selfishness: The Relationship Destroyer

Selfishness can be a subtle yet powerful force that disrupts the delicate balance of relationships. It manifests when you prioritize your own needs and desires over those of others, often at the expense of connection and understanding. Oscar Wilde once remarked, "Selfishness is not living as one wishes to live, it is asking others to live as one wishes to live." This quote encapsulates the essence of selfishness. A tendency to impose your will on others, expecting them to conform to your expectations without considering their perspectives or emotions. In this context, selfishness isn't merely about putting yourself first; it's about disregarding the needs and feelings of those around you. This behavior can create an environment where relationships become transactional rather than reciprocal, stripping away the empathy and mutual respect that form the foundation of meaningful connections.

One of the most insidious forms of selfishness is emotional hoarding where one person in a relationship continuously takes but rarely gives. You may know someone who is always willing to talk about their problems but disappears the moment you need support. Over time, this creates an imbalance that drains the relationship between its energy and goodwill. Imagine a friendship where one person expects to be comforted after every heartbreak or setback but never returns the favor. Eventually, this one-sided dynamic wears thin, and resentment begins to replace connection. The person on the receiving end of this selfish behavior starts to feel like a tool rather than a valued friend, leading to emotional exhaustion and, ultimately, withdrawal.

Studies show that 72% of people cite selfishness as one of the most intolerable traits in relationships (GuidanceTT, 2023). This is because selfish behaviors whether emotional, financial, or practical signal, or a lack of reciprocity, which weakens the foundation of trust in any bond. People naturally seek relationships that feel balanced and supportive, where effort and care are mutually given. When one person repeatedly prioritizes their own interests while neglecting the needs of others, it leads to emotional burnout for those around them.

Selfishness can also appear in more subtle, everyday interactions. It's seen in the friend who constantly dominates conversations, turning every topic back to their own experiences, struggles, or successes. At first, this self-absorption may be excused as enthusiasm or a need for validation, but over time, it becomes a pattern that leaves the other person feeling invisible. People begin to disengage, sensing that they are merely an audience rather than an equal participant in the relationship. The irony is that while the selfish person craves attention and validation, their behavior often leads to the very loneliness they fear.

Another consequence of unchecked selfishness is the erosion of trust and reliability. Relationships thrive on mutual dependability, where both parties feel they can count on each other. But when one person continually puts their convenience first canceling plans at the last minute, failing to follow through on commitments, or always expecting the other person to compromise, trust begins to fracture. Over time, the pattern becomes clear: their needs always take precedence, and others are left feeling unimportant or even disposable. This dynamic makes it difficult for deep friendships to flourish because there is no foundation of reliability or shared effort.

In some cases, selfishness manifests as a lack of consideration for boundaries, creating situations where one person expects the other to be endlessly available, patient, or accommodating. This might be the friend who demands constant reassurance, the family member who refuses to respect personal space, or the partner who only considers their own emotional needs. This type of selfishness can be particularly damaging because it slowly drains the other person's emotional energy, leaving them feeling trapped, guilty, or burdened. When boundaries are consistently ignored, resentment builds, often leading to an eventual rupture in the relationship.

Psychologists suggest that selfishness often stems from a scarcity mindset. The belief that there isn't enough time, love, or success to go around (PsychCentral, 2023). When individuals operate from a place of fear that they might lose out, they hoard emotional energy, focusing solely on their own needs. This perspective distorts relationships, turning them into competitions rather than partnerships. Friendships and romantic relationships that should be built on collaboration instead become battlegrounds for attention and affirmation. Over time, the selfish individual may find themselves increasingly isolated, as others become weary of always playing second fiddle to their ego-driven concerns.

Connecting Insecurity and Selfishness

At first glance, insecurity and selfishness may seem like opposing forces where one is rooted in self-doubt and the other in self-importance. But beneath the surface, they share a common foundation: fear. Insecurity fears rejection, while selfishness fears loss of control. One whispers, "You're not enough," leading to behaviors that seek external validation at any cost. The other demands, "Put yourself first," prioritizing self-preservation over connection. Together, they form a toxic cycle that slowly chips away at relationships.

When insecurity drives behavior, it can lead to self-centered tendencies without the person even realizing it. Consider someone who constantly worries about their place in a friendship. Their fear of being unimportant might push them to dominate conversations, seek constant reassurance, or expect emotional support without reciprocating. To outsiders, this might look like selfishness, but at its core, its insecurity disguised as self-protection. The person isn't trying to be selfish, yet their focus remains on their own emotional needs rather than the balance of the relationship.

On the flip side, selfishness often stems from deep-seated insecurities that haven't been acknowledged or processed. An emotionally unavailable person, dismissive of others' needs, or unwilling to compromise may not necessarily lack care for others. They may simply be afraid of vulnerability. If they open up, they risk being hurt. If they prioritize someone else's needs, they fear losing control. So, they shut people out, focus inward, and ensure their own needs are met first even if it leaves others feeling neglected.

This interplay between insecurity and selfishness is why so many relationships fall apart without either person fully understanding why. One person feels unseen, the other feels unappreciated. One withdraws, and the other demands more. One is afraid to ask for what they need, the other takes too much. The end result? Disconnection, resentment, and loneliness. And perhaps worst of all, both individuals leave feeling misunderstood, believing the other was the problem.

But here's the hard truth: neither insecurity nor selfishness can be "solved" by someone else. No friend, partner, or family member can provide enough validation to erase insecurity, nor can they accommodate selfish behavior enough to make a relationship feel balanced. The real work begins internally recognizing the patterns, identifying the fears that drive them, and challenging the beliefs that keep them alive.

As we move into the next chapter, we'll explore how these destructive patterns start in the mind. The way you talk to yourself, the narratives you repeat, and the standards you hold yourself to can either reinforce insecurity and selfishness or help you break free from them. The first step in creating healthier relationships is recognizing the stories you've been telling yourself and rewriting them.

4

Your Inner Critic Is Lying to You

Picture this: you're standing in front of a mirror, preparing for another day. As you gaze at your reflection, a voice whispers, "You're not good enough," or perhaps, "They don't actually like you." This voice, persistent and insidious, is not the voice of reason or truth. It is your inner critic, a relentless saboteur that often masquerades as your own thoughts. This chapter invites you to meet this inner critic, to unmask the voice that has, for too long, dictated your self-perception and limited your potential. By identifying and understanding this critic, you can begin to dismantle its hold on your life.

Meet the Inner Critic: The Voice That's Not Yours

The inner critic is a master of disguise, often cloaking itself in phrases that seem all too familiar. "You'll never succeed," it might declare, or, "Why even try?" These words are not just fleeting thoughts but deeply ingrained narratives that influence your self-esteem and decision-making. Consider a day when you hesitated to speak up in a meeting, convinced that your ideas lacked value. Or think back to a time you avoided a social gathering, fearing rejection or judgment. These moments are not isolated incidents but echoes of a critical inner voice that has woven itself into the fabric of your daily life, affecting your relationships and choices. This voice thrives on fear and doubt, often louder and more persistent than the whispers of self-assurance and positivity.

Where does this critic come from, you might wonder? Often, its roots stretch back to childhood experiences or societal conditioning. Perhaps it began with a well-intentioned comment from a parent or teacher, meant to guide but instead instilled a sense of inadequacy. These formative experiences lay the groundwork for a self-critical narrative, perpetuated by external pressures and cultural norms.

Society often celebrates achievement and perfection, leaving little room for vulnerability or failure. As you navigate these expectations, the inner critic feeds on perceived shortcomings, growing stronger with each self-doubt. Parental expectations, peer pressure, or cultural ideals can all contribute to the development of self-critical thought patterns. The critic thrives in this environment, reinforcing the belief that you must constantly strive to meet an ever-elusive standard of worthiness.

Brené Brown, a renowned researcher on vulnerability, asks a poignant question: "If you talked to your friends the way you talk to yourself, would you still have friends?" This question serves as a stark reminder of the harshness with which we often treat ourselves. The inner critic is unrelenting, judging our every move with a scrutiny that we would never impose on others. Yet, this self-imposed judgment is not a reflection of reality but a distortion of it, magnifying flaws and minimizing strengths. The critic's voice is not your own but an amalgamation of past criticisms and societal pressures that have been internalized over time. Recognizing this distinction is the first step in reclaiming your narrative and silencing the critic's unjust claims.

Reflection Exercise: Identifying Your Inner Critic

1. **Daily Observation:** Throughout your day, consciously note instances when your inner critic speaks up. What are the specific phrases or criticisms it uses?

2. **Self-Reflection:** Consider the origins of these critical thoughts. Can you trace them back to specific experiences, expectations, or societal norms?

3. **Challenge the Voice:** For each critical thought, write down a counter-argument as if you were defending a friend. What would you say to reassure them?

As you engage with this exercise, you'll start to see patterns in your self-talk, recognizing the critic's pervasive influence.

This awareness is empowering, allowing you to gradually shift the narrative from one of criticism to one of compassion. By unmasking the inner critic, you can begin to reclaim your inner dialogue, fostering a supportive mindset, nurturing, and aligning with your true self. The journey toward self-compassion and acceptance begins here, with the recognition that the critic's voice is not your own and it never has been.

The Lies We Tell Ourselves

The inner critic is a masterful storyteller, crafting narratives that are often rooted not in truth, but in fear and insecurity. Recognizing these false narratives is the first step in reclaiming your self-worth. The critic thrives on exaggeration, taking a small misstep and turning it into a sweeping judgment of character. You might hear, "You'll never be good at this," after a single mistake, or "Everyone thinks you're a fraud," when anxiety creeps in.

These are not truths, but distortions meant to hold you back. To challenge them, cognitive restructuring exercises can be invaluable. This process involves identifying the negative thought, evaluating "its validity, and replacing it with a more balanced perspective" (Spinal-Injury.net, n.d.). Instead of accepting, "I'm a failure," consider, "I made a mistake, and that's part of learning." This shift doesn't happen overnight, but with practice, you can retrain your mind to see setbacks as opportunities rather than confirmations of inadequacy.

Consider Jane, a graphic designer who constantly told herself she wasn't creative enough to succeed. This belief was reinforced every time a project was criticized. But through cognitive restructuring, she began to view criticism as feedback, not a verdict on her talent. By reframing her internal dialogue to, "I can improve with each design," Jane not only enhanced her skills but also built her confidence. Her story illustrates the power of challenging false beliefs and transforming them into steppingstones for growth. Such reframing allows you to see beyond the critic's lies, opening possibilities that once seemed unreachable.

Believing the lies of your inner critic can have profound effects on your life, fueling insecurity and even damaging relationships. When you internalize these false narratives, they can manifest in behaviors that push others away. Negative self-talk often leads to jealousy, as you compare your perceived shortcomings to others' successes. This comparison can foster resentment and envy, creating barriers between you and those you care about.

Similarly, chronic negativity can arise from believing you're not worthy of happiness, affecting not only your mood but also the atmosphere around you. Friends and loved ones might find it difficult to connect when the air is thick with pessimism. Additionally, emotional unavailability can stem from a belief that you're unworthy of love, leading you to shield yourself from vulnerability. This protective mechanism, while intended to guard your heart, often results in isolation.

The quote by Allan Lokos, "Don't believe everything you think. Thoughts are just that—thoughts," underscores the idea that not all thoughts are reflections of reality. It's crucial to remember that thoughts can be fleeting, influenced by emotions or external pressures, and not definitive truths. By holding this perspective, you can begin to discern which thoughts are worth your attention and which are merely echoes of your inner critic. This awareness is vital in breaking the cycle of negativity. It empowers you to question the narratives that drive your actions and emotions, allowing you to choose responses that align with your true values and desires.

As you learn to question your inner critic, you might notice a shift. You'll start to recognize the patterns and triggers that give the critic power. This awareness is a powerful tool, enabling you to disrupt the cycle of self-doubt and replace it with self-compassion. By reframing your thoughts, you open the door to a more authentic and fulfilling life, one where you are not defined by the critic's lies but by your resilience and capacity for growth.

Becoming the Critic's Worst Enemy

To transform the voice of self-criticism into one of support, you must first take control of the narrative. Rewriting your inner dialogue is not about ignoring the negative thoughts but about countering them with affirmations that reflect your true capabilities. Start by creating a "self-compassion mantra." This is a phrase you can repeat during moments of doubt to remind yourself of your worth and potential. Consider something like, "I'm doing the best I can, and that's enough." This mantra serves as a mental anchor, grounding you in self-acceptance and resilience. By consistently reinforcing this positive self-talk, you gradually diminish the power of the inner critic, replacing it with a voice that uplifts and encourages.

Cognitive Behavioral Therapy (CBT) offers practical techniques to reframe negative narratives. This approach involves recognizing when a thought is distorted and challenging its validity. Suppose you find yourself thinking, "I always mess things up." CBT encourages you to examine the evidence: Is this really true? What about the times when you succeeded? This process of cognitive restructuring shifts your perspective, allowing you to see yourself through a more balanced and compassionate lens. It's not about denying your flaws but about acknowledging your strengths and the efforts you make, even when things don't go as planned. This shift in mindset is not instantaneous, but with practice, it becomes a powerful tool against self-doubt.

Practicing self-compassion is crucial in building emotional resilience. Kristin Neff's framework for self-compassion provides a valuable guide. It involves three components: mindfulness, self-kindness, and common humanity. Mindfulness allows you to observe your thoughts and feelings without getting lost in them, creating space for reflection rather than judgment. Self-kindness involves treating yourself with the same warmth and understanding you would offer a friend. This means being gentle with yourself when facing challenges, rather than resorting to harsh criticism. Finally, common humanity reminds you that you are not alone in your struggles. Everyone experiences setbacks and imperfections, and recognizing this shared experience can alleviate feelings of isolation and inadequacy.

To cultivate self-compassion, consider engaging in guided journaling. One effective prompt is: "What would I say to a friend in my situation?" This exercise encourages you to step outside your self-critical mindset and adopt a more empathetic perspective. By writing down supportive words you would offer to someone else, you create a blueprint for how you can speak to yourself in times of need. This practice not only fosters a kinder inner dialogue but also reinforces the habit of self-compassion in your daily life. Over time, these small shifts in how you talk to yourself can lead to significant changes in your self-esteem and emotional well-being.

As you continue to challenge your inner critic, remember that this process requires patience and persistence. It's about gradually building a new narrative, one that honors your efforts and embraces your imperfections. By becoming your inner critic's worst enemy, you open the door to a more authentic and empowered version of yourself, ready to face life's challenges with courage and grace.

The Mindset Shift: Breaking Free from Fixed Thinking

Imagine approaching challenges with an open mind, where setbacks are not personal failures but steppingstones to improvement. This perspective is the essence of embracing a growth mindset. Developed by Carol Dweck, the concept of "a growth mindset encourages the belief that abilities and intelligence can be developed with dedication and hard work." It stands in stark contrast to a fixed mindset, which sees talents as static and unchangeable. When you adopt a growth mindset, you begin to view your shortcomings not as permanent limitations but as opportunities for growth and learning. This shift in thinking can neutralize insecurity and pave the way for healthier relationships, as you become more open to feedback and less threatened by others' successes.

Consider the difference in self-talk when you transition from a fixed to a growth mindset. Instead of saying, "I'm terrible at this," you might find yourself thinking, "I'm learning and improving." This subtle change in language reflects a broader shift in mentality. It acknowledges that effort and persistence can lead to mastery over time. For instance, a colleague who once dreaded public speaking might initially stumble through presentations. But with each attempt, they learn and refine their skills, gradually transforming fear into confidence. This journey exemplifies how a growth mindset fosters resilience and self-acceptance. "It encourages you to embrace challenges, persist in the face of setbacks, and see effort as the path to mastery", rather than a futile endeavor.

Failures, often viewed as the end of the road, can instead be reframed as valuable feedback. They are not definitive judgments on your abilities, but rather opportunities for reflection and growth. Personal stories abound with examples of individuals who turned setbacks into success. Take Thomas Edison, who famously failed thousands of times before inventing the light bulb. Each failure taught him something new, guiding him closer to his goal. His story illustrates the power of perseverance and the ability to learn from mistakes. By adopting this mindset, you can begin to see failures as lessons, each one offering insights that bring you closer to your objectives.

Reflection Exercise: Journaling Lessons from Failures

1. **Reflective Writing:** Choose a past experience where you felt you failed. Write about what happened, focusing on the emotions and thoughts you experienced at the time.

2. **Identify Lessons:** Consider what you learned from this experience. Did it teach you something about your strengths or reveal areas for improvement? Write down any insights gained.

3. **Future Application:** Reflect on how these lessons can inform your future actions. How might you approach similar situations differently, armed with this newfound knowledge?

Engaging in this exercise helps you to distill valuable lessons from past experiences, transforming what once felt like defeat into a source of empowerment. It encourages a mindset that values "growth and learning, fostering resilience in the face of adversity" (OnStoic, n.d.). As you continue to practice this mindset, you'll find that setbacks become less daunting and more manageable, viewed not as roadblocks but as opportunities for growth.

By embracing a growth mindset, you open yourself to a world of possibilities. You learn to appreciate the journey of self-improvement, embracing challenges as opportunities rather than threats. This perspective not only enhances personal growth but also enriches relationships, as you become more open and accepting of both you and others. In this way, a growth mindset becomes a powerful tool for navigating the complexities of life, transforming obstacles into opportunities and challenges into steppingstones toward success.

Taking the Inner Critic to Court

Imagine a courtroom where your inner critic stands accused of distorting your self-image, feeding you a stream of negativity that undermines your confidence. It's time to put this critic on trial, examining its claims with the scrutiny they deserve. Start by considering a critical thought that plagues you. Perhaps, "I'm a bad friend because I forgot their birthday." Gather the evidence. How many times have you been there for them?

Remember the times you listened when they needed an ear or celebrated their successes? This is your evidence, the truth that contradicts the critic's harsh judgment. Challenge the verdict with facts that highlight your loyalty and kindness. This exercise transforms vague accusations into a balanced evaluation, revealing that one oversight does not define your worth. It's about shifting the focus from isolated incidents to a broader perspective of who you are. This approach empowers you to see beyond the critic's narrow lens, embracing a more compassionate and accurate self-view.

As you dismantle the critic's arguments, it's also important to recognize and celebrate your achievements, no matter how small. This practice of acknowledging your successes counters the critic's narrative, building a positive self-image anchored in reality. Consider creating a "win journal." Each day, jot down moments of kindness, courage, or growth.

Perhaps you reached out to a friend, shared a laugh with a colleague, or simply took a moment to breathe and reflect. These wins, though they may seem minor, accumulate over time, painting a picture of resilience and progress. Eckhart Tolle wisely notes, "Acknowledging the good that you already have in your life is the foundation for all abundance." By focusing on these positive aspects, you cultivate a mindset that appreciates the journey of growth, rather than fixating on perceived failures. This practice reinforces your intrinsic value, fostering a sense of accomplishment and self-worth.

The courtroom exercise and win journal are practical tools to reframe your inner dialogue, promoting a balanced and supportive self-image. They remind you that your worth is not determined by fleeting criticisms but by the consistent kindness and effort you bring to your life and relationships. As you continue to challenge your critic and celebrate your wins, you build a foundation of self-compassion and resilience. This foundation supports you as you navigate challenges, bolstering your confidence and encouraging you to pursue your goals with determination.

In the grand scheme of personal growth, these practices are steppingstones toward greater self-awareness and fulfillment. They empower you to engage with the world from a place of confidence, free from the constraints of self-doubt and criticism. By taking your inner critic to court, you reclaim your narrative, embracing the truth of who you are and the potential of who you can become. This chapter sets the stage for further exploration of your inner dialogue, encouraging you to cultivate a mindset that supports your growth and enriches your life.

5

You're Not the Center of the Universe

In the vast tapestry of human connections, it's easy to forget that each thread is part of a larger pattern. We often become entangled in our own narratives, focusing on personal needs and desires, missing the intricate design that surrounds us. However, sometimes this self-focus isn't intentional. It's unconscious self-centeredness, a habit that forms over time without us even realizing it. Recognizing this pattern is essential to fostering meaningful relationships and becoming more present for those around us.

Unconscious self-centeredness doesn't necessarily mean a person is selfish in a malicious way. More often than not, it develops subtly, through routine habits and thought patterns that prioritize personal experiences over the perspectives of others. We all view life through the lens of our own emotions, needs, and struggles, but when this becomes the dominant focus, it can create blind spots in our relationships. Without realizing it, we might dismiss or downplay the feelings of those around us, not because we don't care, but because we are so absorbed in our internal world.

The danger of unconscious self-centeredness is that it often goes unnoticed. Unlike overt arrogance, which is easier to identify and correct, these subtle behaviors manifest as habits interrupting conversations, steering discussions back to ourselves, or assuming that our struggles carry more weight than those of others. Left unchecked, these tendencies can erode relationships, making others feel unheard and undervalued. By becoming aware of how these habits shape our interactions, we take the first step toward shifting our focus outward and strengthening our connections.

Step Outside Yourself

Reflect on your recent interactions. Were they focused on your own experiences, or did they leave space for others? Self-reflection is crucial in recognizing how self-focused tendencies might push people away. Imagine a conversation where you eagerly share your achievements but never ask about the other person's experiences. This oversight can create distance, subtly signaling that their stories are less valuable. If left unchecked, this pattern can make others feel like mere background characters in your life.

Unconscious self-centeredness can take many forms. One subtle example is when someone frequently interrupts conversations, redirecting discussions back to themselves. Another example is emotional monopolization. Always making personal struggles the center of discussion without reciprocating support. While unintentional, these behaviors can be exhausting for friends and family, leading to silent resentment and emotional distance.

A 2020 study from the Journal of Personality and Social Psychology found that individuals who actively practiced perspective-taking developed stronger social bonds and higher emotional intelligence (Galinsky et al., 2020). This means the ability to step outside of yourself isn't just about being polite. It directly impacts the depth and quality of your relationships.

Studies suggest that people who engage in deep, meaningful conversations experience greater emotional fulfillment and stronger relationships (Kashdan & Roberts, 2004). However, unconscious self-centeredness often prevents these deeper connections from forming. When your focus remains on your thoughts, struggles, or successes, you miss opportunities to truly engage with the people around you. The impact of this isn't always immediate, but over time, relationships may weaken, and others may withdraw emotionally, feeling unheard or unvalued.

Recognizing these patterns in yourself is the first step toward change. Many people don't realize how much space they take up in conversations or how often they steer discussions back to themselves. By becoming more aware of these tendencies, you can begin making adjustments that allow for more balanced, reciprocal interactions.

Breaking the Cycle: Practicing Awareness and Connection

Developing self-awareness is the first step toward overcoming unconscious self-centeredness. The following exercises will help you build empathy, strengthen your relationships, and create more meaningful interactions.

Exercise: Shifting Your Focus

1. **Conversation Awareness:** In your next conversation, "make a conscious effort to listen more than you speak" (Broker Solutions, n.d.). Afterward, reflect: Did you focus on their words, or were you mentally preparing your response?

2. **Role-Reversal Reflection:** Think of a recent misunderstanding. Write down your perspective, then attempt to articulate the other person's view. What emotions might they have felt? How did your actions impact them?

3. **The 5-to-1 Rule:** Challenge yourself to ask five meaningful questions before sharing something about yourself in a conversation. This simple habit encourages deeper engagement and mutual exchange.

4. **Silent Observation:** Spend time in a public setting (like a café or park) and observe interactions without judgment. What do you notice about how people engage? This practice helps heighten social awareness.

5. **Empathy Mapping:** When someone shares a challenge, instead of offering advice or turning the focus back to your own experiences, repeat what they said in your own words. This reinforces that you're truly listening.

By incorporating these small but intentional shifts, you begin to replace unconscious self-centeredness with genuine connection. The goal isn't to diminish your own story but to recognize that relationships thrive on balance, reciprocity, and mutual understanding. The more you cultivate this awareness, the stronger and more fulfilling your connections will become.

From Self-Focus to Selfless Connection

Self-centeredness, at its core, can be a formidable barrier to meaningful relationships. It often arises unconsciously, shaped by societal messages that emphasize individualism, personal ambition, or even survival instincts. While focusing on personal goals is not inherently harmful, problems arise when this mindset begins to overshadow our awareness of others. When people become overly absorbed in their own emotions, challenges, or aspirations, they may unintentionally neglect the emotional needs of those around them.

This form of unconscious self-centeredness can manifest in many ways. Consider a friend who only reaches out when they need support but rarely checks in on how you're doing. Or a coworker who dominates team discussions, always prioritizing their ideas without considering input from others. These behaviors, while not always intentional, can gradually wear down trust and connection, creating an emotional imbalance in relationships.

A 2017 study published in the Journal of Social and Personal Relationships found that individuals who regularly reflect on how their actions impact others build stronger, more resilient social bonds (Côté et al., 2017). This highlights the importance of developing an awareness of how our behaviors affect those around us. Shifting from self-focus to selfless connection doesn't mean ignoring personal needs. It means recognizing that relationships thrive when mutual effort and care are present.

One of the most effective ways to counteract self-centered tendencies is through active engagement. Research suggests that people who make a conscious effort to engage in meaningful, reciprocal conversations report greater life satisfaction and deeper friendships (Reis & Clark, 2013). This involves paying attention, listening with intent, and responding in a way that acknowledges the other person's thoughts and emotions rather than waiting for a chance to steer the conversation back to yourself.

Another crucial aspect of fostering connection is acknowledging the emotional experiences of others. Often, people assume they are being empathetic when they offer solutions or share their own similar experiences. However, the true connection doesn't come from fixing someone's problems. It comes from validating their feelings without making the conversation about yourself. A simple but powerful phrase like, "That sounds incredibly difficult. I can only imagine how that must feel," can go a long way in making someone feel heard and valued.

Selfless connection also involves being mindful of how you show up for others. When relationships feel transactional where one person is always giving while the other is always taking, they become unsustainable. Research from the Greater Good Science Center at UC Berkeley shows that acts of generosity and selflessness whether through words, time, or support, strengthen relationships by reinforcing trust and emotional safety (Lyubomirsky, 2013). Small, everyday acts like remembering a friend's important day, offering encouragement, or simply listening without distraction can create lasting bonds.

Ultimately, shifting from self-focus to selfless connection requires intentionality and self-reflection. It's not about abandoning personal ambitions or suppressing your own needs. It's about creating space for others, recognizing that meaningful relationships are built on a foundation of reciprocity, emotional awareness, and shared understanding.

Viewing Challenges as Opportunities

Life is a series of challenges, each presenting an opportunity to learn and grow. Yet, when our focus narrows to ourselves, we often view these challenges as personal affronts rather than shared experiences. This perspective can lead us down a path of blame and isolation, rather than growth and connection. For instance, when disagreements arise, it's easy to see them through a lens of conflict, focusing on who's right and who's wrong. But what if we reframe these disagreements as opportunities to improve communication? By shifting the focus from blame to understanding, we open the door to deeper, more meaningful interactions. This approach not only enhances our relationships but also enriches our emotional intelligence, allowing us to navigate life's complexities with greater ease.

Building resilience through adversity is key to personal and relational growth. Each challenge we face, and each conflict we endure, offers lessons that can strengthen us if we choose to learn from them. Consider the story of a couple who, after countless arguments, decided to view their disagreements as a means to better understand each other. Instead of seeing the conflicts as a sign of failure, they embraced them as a way to grow closer.

They implemented a simple exercise: after each disagreement, they would sit down and write three lessons learned. This practice transformed their relationship, turning challenges into steppingstones toward a deeper connection. It taught them patience, empathy, and the importance of listening, reinforcing the idea that challenges, when viewed through a constructive lens, can build resilience and fortify bonds.

Practical strategies for embracing challenges involve approaching difficulties with a collaborative mindset. One effective method is setting clear, achievable goals that focus on constructive outcomes. When faced with a challenge, whether personal or relational, start by identifying a specific goal. What do you hope to achieve? Break this goal into manageable steps, ensuring each step is realistic and attainable.

This framework not only provides clarity but also fosters a sense of accomplishment as you progress. For example, if you're navigating a challenging relationship, your goal might be to improve communication. The steps could include setting aside time for open discussions, practicing active listening, and seeking feedback. By focusing on collaboration rather than competition, you create an environment where challenges become opportunities for mutual growth and understanding.

Viewing challenges as opportunities requires a shift in perspective, one that values growth over perfection. It invites us to see beyond immediate discomfort, recognizing the potential for learning and transformation. This mindset doesn't eliminate adversity, but it does empower us to face it with courage and resilience. It encourages us to approach life's obstacles not as barriers, but as avenues for personal development and deeper connections with those around us. As we embrace this perspective, we begin to see challenges not as threats, but as integral parts of a fulfilling and meaningful life.

Gratitude Changes Everything

Expressing gratitude is more than a simple exchange of pleasantries; it is a profound practice that can transform your relationships and your life. When you take a moment to express genuine appreciation, you open the door to deeper connections and a more positive outlook. These small gestures, such as a heartfelt thank-you for even the tiniest acts of kindness, make others feel valued and seen. Imagine a colleague who stayed late to help you meet a deadline. A simple "Thank you for your support; it made a big difference" can turn a good working relationship into a great one.

This acknowledgment not only reinforces the positive behavior but also strengthens the bond between you, fostering a sense of mutual respect and appreciation. By focusing on gratitude, you cultivate an environment where positivity thrives, encouraging others to reciprocate the kindness you've shown. This cycle of gratitude and appreciation lays the foundation for lasting connections, where each interaction is imbued with a sense of warmth and understanding.

Incorporating gratitude into your daily routine doesn't require grand gestures; it can be as simple as taking a moment each day to reflect on the things you appreciate. Consider starting a gratitude ritual, where you share one thing, you're thankful for about a friend or partner daily. This practice not only enriches your relationships but also enhances your sense of well-being. By consistently expressing gratitude, you build a strong emotional foundation that supports both personal and relational growth.

Gratitude acts as a lens through which you view the world, shifting your focus from what you lack to what you have. This shift in perspective fosters a mindset of abundance, where you recognize the richness of your life and the people in it. Over time, these daily expressions of gratitude accumulate, weaving a tapestry of connection and joy that envelops your relationships with strength and resilience.

Putting gratitude into action can further solidify these bonds over time. Writing thank-you notes or messages that acknowledge specific things you value about others is a powerful way to deepen your connections. Imagine receiving a note from a friend that says, "I really appreciate how you always make time for me, even when you're busy. It means a lot." Such a message not only uplifts the recipient but also reinforces the bond you share. It reminds them of their importance in your life, strengthening the connection with each word. By taking the time to express gratitude in writing, you create a tangible reminder of the appreciation that exists between you. This act transcends the moment, leaving a lasting impression that nurtures the relationship.

Gratitude is not about taking people for granted, but about noticing and appreciating the role they play in your life. It's about recognizing the small, everyday moments that often go unnoticed like the kind gesture, the supportive word, or the shared laughter. These moments, when acknowledged, become the threads that weave the fabric of your relationships, creating a tapestry rich with meaning and connection. As you practice gratitude, you begin to see the world through a lens of appreciation, where each interaction holds the potential for deeper understanding and connection. This perspective shifts your focus from the transactional to the relational, where the value of each person is recognized and celebrated. In a world where negativity and disconnection often dominate, gratitude serves as a beacon of light, guiding you toward a life filled with warmth, connection, and joy.

Living Fully in the Moment, Together

In our fast-paced, digital world, it's easy to become consumed by the constant barrage of notifications, updates, and virtual interactions, often at the expense of being present with those physically around us. Consider a typical scene: you're sitting with your family or friends, yet your attention drifts to your phone, scrolling through social media. This act, seemingly benign, subtly shifts your focus away from the present, away from the shared experiences unfolding in real time. The moments that could be filled with laughter, meaningful conversations, and deeper connections are instead diluted by distractions. These small instances of divided attention add up, creating invisible walls between you and your loved ones, walls that can only be dismantled through conscious effort and intentional presence.

Practicing mindful presence in relationships demands more than just setting aside technology; it requires a commitment to engage fully with others. Begin by paying attention, not just with your ears, but with your whole being. Make eye contact, a simple yet powerful gesture that conveys interest and respect. Let the other person know you are truly listening, not just waiting for your turn to speak.

This form of mindful listening means being present without formulating your response while the other person is talking. It's about giving the conversation the space it needs to breathe. Reducing distractions during these moments is crucial. Set aside your phone, turn off the television, and create an environment where the focus is solely on the interaction at hand. This undivided attention signals to the other person that they matter, that their thoughts and feelings are valued, fostering a deeper connection.

To cultivate this practice, try an exercise: spend 15 minutes listening to someone without interrupting or thinking of a response. Let their words wash over you, allowing yourself to absorb the nuances of their story. Notice how this changes the dynamic of the conversation, how it invites a flow of understanding and empathy that might otherwise remain untapped. This exercise not only enhances your ability to connect with others but also enriches your own experience, as you learn to appreciate the art of truly being present.

Amid the hustle of daily life, discovering joy in connection often means finding happiness in shared moments and simple experiences. Take a moment to celebrate the small wins together, like acknowledging a friend's achievement or savoring a shared meal. These moments, often overlooked, hold the potential to deepen bonds and create memories rooted in joy and gratitude. Consider the story of two friends who, despite their busy schedules, made it a point to share a cup of coffee each week. This simple ritual became a cherished tradition, a time to reconnect and support each other through life's ups and downs. In these moments, they discovered a profound sense of joy, not in grand gestures, but in the quiet presence of shared companionship.

As we navigate our lives, it's easy to become preoccupied with our own narratives, losing sight of the stories unfolding around us. Yet, by shifting our focus outward, we enhance our connections with others and gain a more in-depth understanding of ourselves. This concept of living fully in the moment, intertwined with the narratives of those around us, sets the stage for exploring the stories we tell ourselves in the next chapter. These stories, whether conscious or subconscious, "shape our identity and influence how we interact with the world" (Black Spring Press, n.d.). As we move forward, let us carry with us the knowledge that true connection lies not in the grand gestures but in the simple, everyday moments that we choose to share with one another.

6

What's Your Story, and Why's It Important

Imagine your life as a book, each chapter filled with experiences that shape who you are. Whether you're aware of them or not, the stories you tell yourself significantly influence your identity and behavior. These narratives, known as "life scripts," are internalized and evolving stories that integrate past experiences, values, beliefs, and aspirations. They help you make sense of your life and define who you are in relation to the world around you. Over time, these stories can enhance your well-being or lead to chaos and sorrow if left fragmented. Understanding the power of your story is crucial, as it provides the structure needed to organize your feelings and experiences, linking your past, present, and future in a cohesive narrative.

These life scripts often originate from early experiences, where family dynamics, trauma, cultural pressures, or significant life events play a pivotal role. For instance, a person frequently criticized during childhood may develop a narrative of being "not good enough." This belief can manifest in adulthood as insecurity-driven behaviors, impacting personal relationships and career choices. Reflect on the messages you absorbed as a child or during challenging moments. What were you told about your worth, capabilities, or place in the world? These messages, whether explicit or implicit, profoundly influence the stories you tell yourself today. They shape how you perceive challenges and opportunities, coloring your interactions with fear or confidence.

To uncover these narratives, engaging in self-discovery is essential. Reflective practices such as journaling can be powerful tools in this process. Consider prompts like, "What are the key events that shaped who I am today?" or "Who was I before the world told me who I should be?" Writing these reflections allows you to trace the origins of your life script, bringing unconscious beliefs to the forefront of your awareness.

Narrative therapy exercises can also help identify recurring patterns and themes in your story. These exercises encourage you to externalize your narrative, examining it as an observer rather than a participant. This shift in perspective can reveal how specific patterns have influenced your decisions and relationships, offering insights into areas where change may be beneficial.

Reflection Exercise: Mapping Your Life Story

- **Event Timeline:** Create a timeline of significant events in your life both positive and negative. Reflect on how each event has contributed to your current narrative.

- **Identifying Themes:** Look for recurring themes or beliefs that emerge from these events. Are there patterns of resilience, fear, or self-doubt?

- **Reframing Exercise:** Consider how you might reinterpret these events. Could a perceived failure be reframed as a learning opportunity? How might this new perspective alter your life script?

These tools for self-discovery not only illuminate the origins of your narrative but also empower you to take control of your story. By understanding and reframing the narratives guiding your life, you can write a script that aligns more closely with your true self and aspirations. This process invites you to challenge limiting beliefs and embrace a narrative that supports growth, resilience, and fulfillment.

How Your Story Shapes Your Behavior

Our narratives about ourselves wield significant power over our actions and beliefs. These personal stories, especially when damaging, can give rise to limiting beliefs and toxic behaviors. Imagine someone who holds the belief, "I'll always be abandoned." This narrative, rooted in past experiences, can lead to emotional unavailability. They might avoid forming deep connections, fearing the inevitable end, even when surrounded by supportive relationships. This self-protective behavior, while understandable, stems from a story that has not been challenged or rewritten. Similarly, consider the belief, "I'm not worthy." This can manifest in people-pleasing tendencies, where the desire for external validation becomes a driving force. Such individuals may neglect their needs, constantly seeking approval from others, leading to chronic negativity and dissatisfaction. These limiting stories not only shape behavior but also reinforce a cycle of self-doubt and insecurity.

The mental health impact of these limiting stories is profound. When personal narratives are tied to painful experiences, they act as cognitive biases, filtering new experiences to confirm old beliefs. Imagine filtering every interaction through a lens of unworthiness, perceiving neutral or even positive events as further evidence of inadequacy. This bias distorts reality, making it difficult to recognize genuine achievements or positive feedback.

Brené Brown wisely states, "The stories we tell ourselves shape the lives we live." This insight highlights the necessity of recognizing and altering these narratives. By understanding how stories influence mental well-being, you can start to challenge the biases that perpetuate a cycle of negativity. Recognizing these patterns allows for the possibility of rewriting your story, shifting the focus from limitation to potential.

Your story doesn't just affect your self-view; it extends into your relationships, influencing how you interact with others. Reflecting on moments of conflict can reveal the underlying narratives that drive your actions. Ask yourself, "What belief about myself was I protecting?" This question uncovers the deeper story beneath surface-level reactions.

Perhaps a heated argument with a friend was less about the disagreement and more about a fear of rejection rooted in childhood experiences. By identifying these connections, you can address the real issue, leading to more authentic and open interactions. For instance, if you find yourself avoiding confrontation, it may be because your story equates conflict with rejection. Recognizing this allows you to challenge that narrative, opening the door to healthier communication.

Engaging in reflective exercises can help you connect your current actions to these negative narratives. Consider a recent conflict, what was the underlying belief driving your response? Write it down and examine its origins. Is it a belief that serves you well, or is it a remnant of past experiences that no longer applies? This introspection can be revealing, allowing you to pinpoint the areas where your story needs revision.

As you uncover these connections, you gain the power to change your narrative, transforming behaviors that once seemed set in stone. This process is about more than just understanding; it's about taking action to create a narrative that aligns with your true self and aspirations. By doing so, you free yourself from the constraints of outdated stories, paving the way for growth and fulfillment in all aspects of life.

Breaking Free: Challenging Your Limiting Beliefs

Limiting beliefs are those invisible barriers that quietly "shape our lives, often without our conscious awareness" (The Matrix of Destiny, n.d.). These beliefs act as silent saboteurs, stemming from deeply ingrained negative narratives. They whisper insidious messages like, "I'm not lovable," "I don't deserve success," or

"Everyone will hurt me." Such beliefs confine us within invisible walls, dictating our actions and reactions. They are not truths, yet they feel undeniable, casting shadows over our potential and happiness.

As you navigate life, these beliefs can become so entrenched that they seem like absolutes, leading to patterns of behavior that reinforce their hold. For example, if you've ever thought, "I must always win," it might stem from a fear of inadequacy. This belief could manifest in selfish actions, making it difficult to admit fault, even when doing so would foster growth and understanding.

These limiting beliefs often reinforce toxic behaviors, becoming the undercurrent that drives actions detrimental to relationships. Consider how jealousy, manipulation, or overstepping boundaries might emerge from these beliefs. A person convinced that they must always come out on top may act in ways that prioritize their success over others, even at the expense of fairness and empathy.

This needs to assert dominance can strain friendships and partnerships, creating an environment where trust and mutual respect wither. The struggle to admit fault or vulnerability, fueled by the belief that showing weakness equals failure, "can lead to a cycle of defensiveness" and blame (Parent Portfolio, n.d.). Such behaviors, while protective in intent, often lead to isolation and further entrenchment of the very beliefs one seeks to escape.

Recognizing these limiting beliefs is the first step toward liberation. Begin by engaging in self-assessment. Ask yourself, "What recurring thoughts hold me back?" Consider journaling as a tool to capture these thoughts, allowing you to see patterns that may not be apparent in the moment. This process helps externalize internal dialogues, making it easier to identify which beliefs serve you and which hinder your growth. Cognitive Behavioral Therapy (CBT) techniques can be particularly effective in challenging these automatic negative thoughts. CBT encourages questioning the validity of these beliefs, examining evidence for and against them, and gradually replacing them with more balanced thoughts. This practice doesn't require professional intervention; it begins with curiosity and a willingness to explore your mental landscape.

Replacing limiting beliefs with empowering ones requires intention and practice. Start with positive affirmations, simple yet powerful statements that counter negative self-talk. Instead of "I'm not good enough," try saying, "I am growing and improving every day." This affirmation acknowledges your journey while celebrating progress, however small. Reframing past experiences is another technique. Look at setbacks not as failures, but as opportunities for learning and resilience. Visualizing success can also be transformative. "Picture yourself achieving your goals, feeling the emotions associated with success", and living in alignment with your true values (Findzhikov, 2024). This mental rehearsal strengthens new beliefs, making them feel more attainable and real.

Interactive Exercise: Rewriting Limiting Beliefs

- **Identify a Limiting Belief:** Write down a belief that frequently holds you back.

- **Challenge and Reframe:** List evidence that contradicts this belief. Reflect on times you succeeded or proved this belief wrong.

- **Create a New Affirmation:** Develop a positive statement to replace the limiting belief. Repeat this affirmation daily, integrating it into your self-talk.

By engaging in this exercise, you begin to dismantle the barriers that these beliefs have built over time. This process is not about denying your experiences but about reinterpreting them in a way that fosters growth and self-compassion. As you replace limiting beliefs with empowering ones, you open doors to new possibilities, transforming your narrative from one of constraint to one of potential and hope.

The Science of Rewriting Memories

Memory, far from being a static record, is a dynamic, ever-changing construct. Our minds continuously reconstruct memories, making them adaptable and sometimes unreliable. This malleability means that memories can be reshaped, altered by new information, or even distorted over time.

Elizabeth Loftus, a renowned cognitive psychologist, has extensively studied how our memories can be influenced and reshaped, demonstrating that they are not as infallible as we might believe. Her research highlights how memories, particularly those laden with emotion, can be susceptible to change. This adaptability can be both a challenge and an opportunity. While our recollections can lead us astray, they also offer a pathway to healing and transformation. Understanding this flexibility allows us to explore how past experiences have been woven into our identities, often shaping the stories we tell about ourselves in ways that may no longer serve us.

Negative memories can give rise to toxic stories that haunt us, fueling insecurities and toxic behaviors long after the original events have passed. Consider a childhood moment of public humiliation, perhaps during a school play or a classroom event. The sting of that experience might imprint a lifelong fear of rejection or public speaking. Each subsequent situation that triggers a similar emotion reinforces this narrative, creating a self-fulfilling prophecy of avoidance and anxiety.

These unresolved painful memories act as anchors, tethering us to outdated scripts that dictate our responses in the present. They can lead to patterns of behavior that perpetuate feelings of inadequacy, making it challenging to break free from cycles of self-doubt and fear. It is within this context that the science of memory reconstruction offers hope. By acknowledging the fluid nature of memory, "we can begin to challenge and reframe these narratives", opening the door to change and growth (Inspiration Power Boost, n.d.).

Rewriting memories involves practical techniques that can transform the emotional impact of specific events. Guided imagery is one such tool, allowing you to revisit a memory and alter its emotional tone. Imagine returning to that childhood moment of failure, but this time, envision it with a supportive audience, perhaps with a mentor or friend offering encouragement. This reimagined scenario can help diminish the memory's emotional charge, reducing its power over your current self-perception. Another effective exercise is writing a letter to your younger self.

In this letter, reinterpret the event with empathy and kindness, acknowledging the feelings of the time while offering wisdom and reassurance from your current perspective. This practice fosters self-compassion, enabling you to view past challenges as steps along your path rather than defining moments. By engaging in these exercises, you begin to rewrite the script, allowing yourself to move beyond the constraints of past narratives.

The benefits of reframing past experiences are profound, leading to emotional healing and significant behavioral change. Case studies abound of individuals who have turned painful memories into catalysts for growth. Consider someone who once feared public speaking due to a childhood embarrassment. Through memory rewriting techniques, they may come to view that event as a pivotal learning experience, one that ultimately spurred them to develop resilience and confidence. By reframing the narrative, they transform a source of fear into a wellspring of strength.

This shift not only alters their self-perception but also impacts their interactions and choices, leading to more fulfilling and authentic engagements with the world. The ability to reinterpret memories allows for a reimagining of identity, where past adversities are seen not as barriers but as formative experiences that contribute to a richer, more complex sense of self. This process of rewriting memories and narratives opens possibilities for healing, empowering you to step into a future unburdened by the constraints of your past.

Creating a Vision for Your Future

Crafting a vision for your future acts as a beacon, guiding you through the uncertainties of life. It serves as a motivational tool, helping you transcend past limitations and focus on what truly matters. By envisioning a future where you have moved beyond self-doubt and fear, you empower yourself to make decisions aligned with your aspirations. This clarity transforms limiting beliefs into steppingstones, allowing you to build a life rich with meaning and purpose. People who have reframed their limiting beliefs often find themselves capable of achieving more than they ever imagined. They see potential where they once saw obstacles, crafting a life narrative driven by possibilities rather than constraints.

To create this vision, begin with actionable exercises designed to help you imagine your future self. Consider making a vision board. A visual tapestry of your goals and aspirations. Select images and words that resonate with your dreams, arranging them on a board to serve as a daily reminder of where you want to go. This tangible representation helps solidify your intentions, making your goals feel more achievable. Reflect on questions such as, "What kind of relationships, career, and life do I want to build?"

Dive deep into these reflections, allowing your mind to explore various scenarios and possibilities. This process isn't just about setting goals; it's about understanding the essence of what fulfillment means to you. Through this exploration, you begin to paint a picture of a future that excites and motivates you.

Aligning your actions with this vision involves integrating your new narrative into everyday habits and decisions. Break down your long-term vision into realistic, short-term steps that you can take today. For instance, if your new story is "I'm worthy of strong relationships," start by reaching out to loved ones, expressing gratitude, or setting healthy boundaries that honor your needs.

Each small action reinforces your vision, creating "a positive feedback loop that builds momentum over time" (Fly Bodies, n.d.). As you take these steps, be mindful of how they contribute to your overall narrative. Celebrate each milestone, recognizing that every effort, no matter how small, brings you closer to your desired future. This incremental approach not only makes your vision more manageable but also cultivates a sense of accomplishment and progress.

Staying open to change is crucial as your vision evolves. Life is unpredictable, and your goals may shift as you grow and learn. Embrace adaptability, understanding that flexibility is not a deviation from your path but a natural part of growth. Consider the words, "Dreams don't have deadlines; they have directions." This perspective allows you to adjust your vision without losing sight of your core values and aspirations. Stories abound of individuals who have adjusted their visions to overcome life's challenges.

These stories illustrate the power of resilience and adaptability, showing how a flexible approach can lead to unexpected opportunities and successes. By remaining open to change, you allow your vision to evolve in harmony with your personal growth, ensuring that it remains relevant and inspiring.

As you create and refine your vision, remember that it is a living, breathing entity. It reflects not only who you are but who you are becoming. This chapter has explored the transformative power of vision, guiding you to imagine and build a future that aligns with your true self. With clarity and intentionality, you can transcend past limitations and step confidently into a life of possibility and fulfillment. In the next chapter, we will delve into the art of self-love, exploring how embracing your authentic self can deepen your connections and enrich your journey.

7

Rewriting New Stories

In the realm of self-discovery, the narratives we hold about ourselves often dictate the paths we tread and the limits we impose. These stories, woven from past experiences and internalized beliefs, can either empower us or trap us in cycles of self-doubt and negative thinking. Picture your mind as a canvas, painted with narratives shaped over time. Some vibrant and full of potential while others shadowed by fear and insecurity.

It's easy to let the darker hues dominate, but what if you had the power to repaint the canvas, to rewrite the story of your life? This chapter invites you to explore the art of narrative transformation, empowering you to shed the constraints of negative self-talk and embrace a narrative that reflects your true potential.

Learning to Love the Real You

Negative stories often hold us back, rooted in "cognitive distortions that skew our perception of reality" and our self-worth (Hinks, n.d.). These distortions, as described by David Burns in his research on cognitive therapy, act like filters, allowing only negative aspects of experiences to pass through while ignoring the positive. For instance, overgeneralization can lead you to believe that a single failure defines your entire existence, while polarized thinking reduces life's complexities to black-and-white extremes. These distortions create a narrative where you constantly tell yourself, "I'll never be good enough," trapping you in a cycle of self-doubt and limiting your ability to grow.

Understanding these cognitive distortions is the first step toward rewriting your story. A study in the Journal of Cognitive Therapy and Research (Beck, 2016) found that individuals who learned to identify and challenge distorted thoughts showed higher levels of self-confidence and resilience. Recognizing these patterns helps dismantle limiting beliefs and creates space for new, empowering perspectives.

Instead of merely identifying negative thoughts, actively replacing them with balanced perspectives is key. Consider this shift: Instead of "I always fail," try, "I struggled with this before, but I've succeeded in other areas I can improve." The goal isn't blind optimism but realistic self-compassion, acknowledging challenges without allowing them to define your worth.

One way to reinforce this shift is by rewriting your internal script. If you've always thought, I'm not capable of achieving my goals, try reframing it as I am building my skills and making progress every day. This subtle adjustment doesn't ignore difficulties but reframes them as part of your growth journey rather than a barrier to success.

A powerful tool for rewriting your inner narrative is self-affirmation journaling. Research from Personality and Social Psychology Review (Steele, 2010) suggests that self-affirmations help reduce stress and increase resilience by reinforcing a positive self-concept. Writing down daily affirmations that align with your values can help reshape your mindset over time.

Interactive Exercise: Rewriting Negative Narratives

To integrate this new way of thinking, practice the following:

1. **Catch & Challenge Negative Thoughts**
   - Identify a recurring negative thought. Example: I always mess things up.
   - Ask: Is this 100% true? What evidence contradicts this?
   - Rewrite it: I have made mistakes, but I have also learned and succeeded in many areas.
2. **Rewrite Your Story as a Growth Narrative**
   - Write down a challenge you've faced and how you originally interpreted it.
   - Now, rewrite it from a perspective of growth: What did you learn? How did you become stronger?

3. **Daily Affirmation Writing**
   - Each day, write one sentence affirming a new belief about yourself.
   - Example: Instead of I'm not good at relationships, write I am learning to communicate better and build healthy connections.

By engaging in these practices, you begin the process of reshaping your self-story, moving away from limiting beliefs and toward a mindset that celebrates progress, resilience, and self-worth.

Celebrating Small Wins

In a world that often magnifies our failures and minimizes our successes, the power of positive reinforcement can be transformative. It's easy to overlook the small victories that punctuate our daily lives, yet these seemingly insignificant achievements hold the key to rewiring our brains and reshaping our self-perception. Imagine your mind as a fertile garden, where each small win is a seed planted with care.

As these seeds take root, they cultivate a landscape of positivity and growth, challenging the negative narratives that have long held you captive. By shifting your focus to these accomplishments, you train your mind to recognize progress rather than dwelling on perceived failures.

Positive reinforcement is more than just a feel-good strategy; it's a powerful psychological tool that can help reinforce desired behaviors and thoughts. According to B.F. Skinner's operant conditioning model, positive reinforcement involves introducing a desirable stimulus following a behavior to increase the likelihood of that behavior being repeated.

In the context of personal growth, this means recognizing and celebrating small achievements to encourage further progress. Each time you acknowledge a victory, no matter how minor, you send a signal to your brain that reinforces positive self-talk and encourages continued effort. Over time, this practice can shift your mindset, helping you to see yourself as capable and resilient.

Consider the value of reflecting on your day and identifying one small thing you did well. This practice, though simple, can have profound effects on your self-esteem and motivation. Perhaps you managed to complete a challenging task at work or showed kindness to a stranger. Maybe you took a step toward a personal goal or practiced self-care despite a busy schedule. Whatever it is, take a moment to celebrate it.

Acknowledging these small wins not only boosts your confidence but also creates a positive feedback loop that encourages further success. By focusing on what you've done right, you gradually diminish the power of self-doubt and cultivate a mindset of growth and possibility.

Creating a positive evidence list is an effective way to document and reinforce these small wins, providing tangible proof that challenges negative beliefs. Start by keeping a journal dedicated to your accomplishments. Each day, write down at least one achievement, no matter how small. Over time, this journal becomes a powerful tool for combating negative thoughts. When self-doubt creeps in, you can refer back to your list, reminding yourself of the progress you've made and the potential that lies within you. This practice not only shifts your focus from failure to success but also builds a reservoir of positive experiences to draw upon in moments of uncertainty.

The act of documenting small wins serves as a form of positive reinforcement, strengthening your belief in your ability to achieve and grow. It challenges the pervasive narrative of inadequacy, replacing it with a story of resilience and strength. As you review your journal, you'll begin to see patterns of growth and development, reinforcing your capacity for change and adaptation. This practice is particularly powerful for individuals who struggle with low self-esteem or who tend to overthink, as it provides concrete evidence of their capabilities and achievements.

For instance, imagine a scenario where you're faced with a daunting project at work. As you progress, you encounter setbacks and moments of doubt. In these instances, your positive evidence list becomes an invaluable resource. By reflecting on past successes, you remind yourself that you've overcome challenges before and are capable of doing so again. This reflection not only boosts your confidence but also provides the motivation needed to persist in the face of adversity. It shifts your focus from what's daunting to what's achievable, reinforcing a narrative of empowerment and possibility.

While the concept of celebrating small wins may seem simplistic, its impact is profound. By consistently acknowledging your achievements, you cultivate a mindset of positivity and growth, challenging the negative beliefs that have long held you back. This practice is not about ignoring challenges or failures but about recognizing the progress you've made and the potential that lies ahead. It's about shifting your focus from what you lack to what you possess, from what's gone wrong to what's going right. In doing so, you create a narrative of resilience and strength, one that empowers you to face life's challenges with confidence and courage.

As you incorporate this practice into your daily routine, you'll begin to notice subtle shifts in your mindset and self-perception. You'll find yourself more attuned to opportunities for growth and less focused on obstacles. You'll begin to see yourself not as a person defined by limitations, but as someone capable of achieving and thriving. By celebrating your small wins, you pave the way for larger victories, transforming your narrative from one of self-doubt to one of self-belief. This shift is not only empowering but also liberating, freeing you from the constraints of negative thinking and opening the door to a future filled with possibility and potential.

Respect Yourself Enough to Rewrite Your Story

So far, we've explored how the stories you tell yourself shape your beliefs and how small wins reinforce a positive mindset. Now, it's time to take action. Unlike the previous sections, this part of the chapter is structured with clear, actionable steps to help you rewrite your narrative and align your new beliefs with real change.

In the quiet moments of introspection, when you're alone with your thoughts, it's easy to become ensnared by the web of negative beliefs that have settled into the corners of your mind. These core beliefs, like "I'm unlovable" or "I'll never be successful," often take root early in life, nurtured by past experiences and reinforced over time. They become part of your identity, subtly shaping your decisions, relationships, and self-worth. Yet, recognizing these beliefs as mental constructs rather than unshakable truths is the first step toward reclaiming your narrative.

However, rewriting your story isn't just about changing your thoughts. It's about taking action that reinforces new beliefs and aligns with the life you want to create. It's one thing to say, "I am worthy of success," but unless your daily actions support this belief, it remains just a thought. True transformation happens when your mindset and behaviors begin working together, reinforcing your new narrative through consistent action.

1. Aligning Your Actions with Your New Narrative

Living out your rewritten story requires deliberate choices and not just internal shifts, but external changes that mirror your new self-concept. Think of it like rewriting a script: If you've always played the role of "the one who never speaks up," you don't just change the internal dialogue, you actively practice voicing your thoughts in conversations. Every small action reinforces the reality of your new narrative.

To make this shift tangible, start by setting small, achievable goals that align with your rewritten beliefs:

- If your new story is "I am capable of success," your first action might be tackling one small project you've been avoiding.
- If your story is "I am worthy of love and connection," your action might be reaching out to a friend without fear of rejection.
- If your story is "I am strong and resilient," your step could be facing a difficult conversation instead of avoiding it.

These small, intentional choices create momentum, proving to your mind (and reinforcing to your subconscious) that your new belief is not just an abstract idea. It's a reality you are actively building.

2. Breaking Free from Old Habits & Patterns

One challenge of rewriting your narrative is breaking old habits that reinforce limiting beliefs. Your brain is wired for efficiency, meaning it will default to what's familiar. Even if those familiar patterns are harmful. Overcoming this requires intentional habit-building strategies:

1. Change Your Environment to Support New Habits

Your surroundings influence your behaviors. If you want to adopt a new mindset, make physical adjustments to your space that reflect this shift.

- Want to believe you are confident? Adjust your posture, make eye contact, and speak with certainty.
- Want to feel motivated? Surround yourself with reminders such as notes, books, or vision boards that rcinforce your goals.
- Want to believe you are worthy of rest? Set up a calming nighttime routine that prioritizes self-care.

2. Replace Negative Self-Talk with Pattern Interrupts

If an old belief creeps in I'll never succeed, use a pattern interrupt:

- Say "Stop!" out loud or visualize a red stop sign.
- Immediately follow with an empowering statement that aligns with your new story (I am learning and growing every day).
- Pair this with a small action, like taking a deep breath or adjusting your posture, to physically reinforce the shift.

3. Create Rituals That Reinforce Your New Identity

Your identity is shaped by consistent habits. If your new story is "I am resilient and adaptable," reinforce it with rituals that remind you of your strength. This could be journaling about challenges you've overcome, adopting a daily mantra, or practicing micro-bravery taking one small risk each day to step outside your comfort zone.

By making these intentional behavioral shifts, you send a clear message to yourself: This isn't just an idea, it's who I am becoming.

3. Embracing Growth While Letting Go of Perfection

One of the biggest obstacles in rewriting your story is the fear of not getting it right. Many people hesitate to step into a new identity because they believe they must be perfect at it from the start. But rewriting your story isn't about perfection, it's about progress.

You will have setbacks. You might find yourself slipping into old thought patterns. You may still hear echoes of doubt. That doesn't mean you've failed. It means you're human, and growth is an ongoing process.

The key is to approach this journey with self-compassion:

- When setbacks happen, ask yourself: What can I learn from this? Instead of Why do I always mess up?
- Instead of expecting instant change, focus on tiny shifts over time. One choice, one decision, or one action at a time.
- Celebrate progress, no matter how small. Every step forward is proof that your story is evolving.

The real success isn't in never struggling, it's in continuing to move forward despite the struggles.

4. Your Story is Yours to Write

Rewriting your story is not about erasing the past but reframing it in a way that empowers you. Your experiences may have shaped you, but they do not define you. You have the power to reshape your narrative into one of resilience, growth, and self-worth.

As you continue this journey, remember:

- Your new story becomes real through action, not just thought.
- Change is built on small, daily choices that reinforce your new beliefs.
- Growth isn't about perfection, it's about persistence.

In the next chapter, we'll explore self-love as a foundation for lasting change. Because once you learn to rewrite your story, the next step is embracing the unshakable truth that you are worthy of the life you are building.

8

Falling in Love with Yourself

Imagine for a moment standing on the threshold of a vast and untamed wilderness, a place where the only path is the one you carve for yourself. This wilderness represents the uncharted territory of your true self, a landscape rich with the potential of who you are beyond the expectations of the world. Yet, the journey to this place is often fraught with apprehension, as many of us have been conditioned to hide behind masks, shaped by insecurities and fears of judgment.

These masks, while offering the illusion of protection, can obscure the true essence of who we are, leaving us disconnected from our authentic selves. Embracing the journey to self-discovery is about removing these masks, unearthing the layers that conceal our unique qualities, and finding freedom in authenticity.

Discover the You That's Been Waiting

In a world that often celebrates extroversion and outspokenness, those who are more introspective may feel compelled to hide their true nature. This societal bias often pushes people to wear masks, concealing their authentic selves to fit in. Consider the child labeled as "too quiet," who grows up suppressing their introspective tendencies, mistaking them for flaws. Over time, this child adapts to external expectations, losing touch with the rich inner world that defines them. These masks, while seemingly protective, can distance us from the freedom of being who we truly are. Real liberation comes from acknowledging these barriers, understanding their roots, and shedding them to embrace authenticity.

Reconnecting with your inner self requires rediscovering the passions, values, and traits that make you unique. These elements act as a compass, guiding you toward a life aligned with your true self. Start by reflecting on this question: "If you stripped away who others expect you to be, who would you become?" This process of introspection is a powerful tool that illuminates the path back to your authentic self. As you consider this question, think about the activities, values, and memories that bring joy and fulfillment. These reflections reveal the core elements of your identity, offering a roadmap to rediscover and embrace your true self.

Passion Inventory Exercise:

1. **Activities:** What hobbies or interests ignite excitement within you? Identify activities you may have set aside to conform to societal norms.

2. **Values:** What deeply held principles guide your decisions? Reflect on how your daily actions align or don't align with these values.

3. **Memories:** Recall moments of happiness and fulfillment. What do these memories reveal about what truly matters to you?

Use this inventory as a living document. Return to it often, adding new insights as you continue exploring and honoring your true self.

The decision to fully accept yourself marks a profound emotional transformation. It is a declaration of self-love. An acknowledgment that every part of you, flaws included, is deserving of respect and admiration. Oscar Wilde encapsulated this beautifully: "To love oneself is the beginning of a lifelong romance." This romance is not rooted in vanity but in nurturing the most enduring relationship you will ever have. The one with yourself.

Consider the story of a woman who spent years chasing external validation, believing her worth was tied to the opinions of others. Only when she embraced her imperfections and stopped seeking approval did she find true peace. This internal shift empowered her to approach life with authenticity, forging deeper connections and experiencing joy unburdened by external expectations.

As you embark on this journey of self-discovery, remember that falling in love with yourself is not a singular event but a continuous process. It involves embracing all aspects of who you are, including the parts you've hidden away or judged harshly.

Self-love is not about achieving perfection. It's about recognizing the beauty of your imperfections and seeing them as integral to your identity. By cultivating this relationship with yourself, you "pave the way for deeper, more authentic connections with others", as self-love naturally enhances empathy and trust (Khkitab, n.d.).

Quiet the Noise and Listen to Your Heart

In a world filled with constant chatter and countless opinions, the voice of your inner critic can be incredibly loud. This critic thrives on negative self-talk, undermining your confidence and feeding your doubts. It whispers that you're not capable, that failure is imminent, and that others are far better. To confront this voice, begin by personifying it. Give it a name, perhaps something whimsical or even absurd, like "Grumpy Gus" or "Naggy Nancy."

By doing so, you diminish its power, transforming it from a menacing presence into something you can manage. Imagine catching yourself thinking, "I'll fail anyway." Instead, respond to this thought as if addressing a pesky companion: "Grumpy Gus, I'm learning and growing from every step I take." This shift not only counters negativity but also reclaims your narrative, turning self-doubt into a platform for growth.

Rewriting your internal dialogue is a transformative act that builds self-love and confidence over time. Positive affirmations serve as potent tools in this process, reshaping the way you perceive yourself. Consider incorporating affirmations that resonate with your core beliefs, such as "I am worthy, I am capable, I am enough." Repeat these daily, allowing them to seep into your consciousness and replace deeply ingrained limiting beliefs. This practice is more than mere repetition; it's an act of reprogramming your mind to embrace positivity.

Engage in a simple exercise: whenever a negative thought arises, write it down. Then, immediately rewrite it into a positive alternative. For instance, transform "I'm not good enough" into "I am learning and improving every day." This exercise not only alters your mindset but also cultivates resilience, empowering you to face challenges with newfound confidence.

Listening to your heart amidst the external noise requires intentional practice. It involves discerning between the cacophony of expectations placed on you by others and the authentic desires that resonate within. Allocate ten minutes each day to sit in silence, observing your thoughts and feelings without judgment. This practice fosters a deeper connection with your inner self, allowing you to identify what truly matters to you. As you engage in this introspective silence, pay attention to the desires that emerge. Are they driven by your aspirations, or do they stem from societal pressures? Understanding this distinction is key to aligning your life with your authentic self.

Tuning into your heart means embracing the courage to pursue your dreams, even when they diverge from the paths others expect you to follow. It's about honoring your unique journey and trusting that your desires are valid and worth pursuing.

This process of quieting external noise and listening to your heart cultivates self-awareness, empowering you to live authentically and fully. As you continue to practice self-reflection and positive self-talk, you'll find that the voice of doubt gradually diminishes, replaced by a chorus of self-assurance and acceptance. In this space, you begin to thrive, discovering a profound sense of peace and fulfillment.

Dance With Your Flaws, Not Against Them

In the realm of self-discovery, flaws often appear as obstacles to overcome. Yet, these imperfections are not barriers; they are bridges to authenticity. They add depth, creating a unique texture to your being. Consider the trait of introversion. Society might view it as a limitation, a reason to shy away from social interactions. However, introversion can also be a gateway to profound introspection and observation.

It allows for deeper connections and a more thoughtful approach to life. Flaws, then, are not failures. They are indicators of growth, evidence that you are human, continually evolving. Embracing these aspects of yourself creates a richer, more nuanced self-perception. One that celebrates your journey rather than fixating on perceived shortcomings.

Progress, rather than perfection, is the true measure of self-growth. Transitioning from judgment to celebration is a transformative exercise in self-love. Instead of focusing on flaws as deficits, recognize how far you've come in embracing them. Start by identifying three aspects of yourself that you once considered shortcomings. Reflect on the progress you've made in reframing these traits or how they've contributed to your personal development. For example, if you've always thought of yourself as "overthinking," you might now see it as a strength for thorough decision-making. This exercise isn't about rewriting your story overnight but about honoring the milestones that shape your growth.

Celebrating personal victories, no matter how small, reinforces this mindset. Keep a "progress journal" where you document moments of growth. Did you handle a situation with more confidence than before? Did you offer yourself grace instead of self-criticism after a mistake? These moments, while seemingly minor, signify your evolution. Over time, tracking these milestones fosters a sense of pride in your journey and shifts your focus from what's "missing" to what's flourishing.

Personal development is not a destination; it's a dynamic and ongoing process. Each step forward is a testament to your resilience and willingness to grow. Consider the journey of Oprah Winfrey, who turned early struggles into a foundation for empowerment. Her ability to channel adversity into purpose illustrates that imperfections can be powerful catalysts for transformation. When you view progress through this lens, even the smallest steps forward become victories worth celebrating.

Embracing your flaws is an invitation to dance with the rhythm of your growth. It's not about erasing imperfections but about weaving them into the tapestry of your unique story. This process fosters self-compassion and encourages a holistic understanding of your identity. By celebrating each step of your journey, you cultivate a mindset that values growth over perfection. In doing so, you create space for your true self to flourish, grounded in authenticity and self-love.

Turn Self-Care Into a Love Language

Imagine self-care not as a luxury but as a necessary and deliberate act of love for yourself. This perspective transforms it from indulgence to an essential practice that honors your needs, allowing you to present your best self to the world. By nurturing yourself, you cultivate the energy and resilience needed to navigate life's challenges. Picture self-care as treating yourself with the same kindness and consideration you would offer a cherished loved one.

This means preparing nourishing meals that fuel your body, taking time to rest and recharge, and "engaging in creative pursuits that bring joy and fulfillment" (Anaadi, n.d.). These actions are not selfish; they are vital to maintaining your well-being and ensuring that you can be fully present in all aspects of your life. By redefining self-care as an expression of love, you shift your perception, recognizing it as a fundamental component of a balanced and fulfilling life.

Creating rituals that nurture your body, and mind involves developing daily practices that align with your emotional, mental, and physical needs. These rituals serve as anchors, grounding you amidst the chaos of everyday life. Consider beginning your day with a moment of "meditation, allowing yourself to center your thoughts and set positive intentions" (Commissiong, 2024).

Gratitude journaling can be another powerful practice, helping you focus on the positive aspects of your life and fostering a mindset of abundance. Physical movement, whether a brisk walk, yoga session, or dance, invigorates your body and releases endorphins that uplift your mood. The key is to treat these self-care activities with the same priority as any important appointment. By scheduling them into your day, you create a structured routine that supports your well-being and reinforces the importance of self-care in your life. This commitment to nurturing yourself not only enhances your quality of life but also strengthens your capacity to support and connect with others.

Protecting your peace requires setting boundaries and prioritizing your well-being without guilt. It means recognizing your limits and honoring them, even when others may not understand. Practice saying "no" gracefully when necessary. A simple, "I'd love to help, but I can't commit right now," is an empowering way to assert your needs while maintaining respect for the other person. Setting boundaries is not about shutting others out; it's about creating a safe space where you can thrive.

Reflect on the question, "What boundaries do I need to set to protect my energy and peace?" This reflection invites you to consider the areas of your life where your well-being may be compromised and to take proactive steps to safeguard your mental and emotional health. By prioritizing your needs, you create an environment where you can flourish without the weight of external pressures. This practice of self-respect and boundary-setting fosters a sense of empowerment, enabling you to engage with the world from a place of strength and authenticity.

Build a Forever Relationship With Yourself

Imagine the profound connection you can cultivate when you recognize yourself as your greatest companion. This relationship is the longest and most meaningful you will ever have, for it is with the one person who will accompany you through every moment of life: yourself. Wayne Dyer once said, "You cannot be lonely if you like the person you're alone with." This speaks to the transformative power of self-acceptance.

When you enjoy your own company, solitude becomes a space for rejuvenation rather than loneliness. Time spent alone turns into an opportunity for reflection, creativity, and growth. In solitude, the noise of the world fades, allowing you to hear your thoughts and desires with clarity. This shift in perception allows you to embrace solitude as a nurturing environment where you can develop your inner landscape and strengthen your sense of self.

Every day presents a new opportunity to show up for yourself by keeping promises that build self-trust and confidence. These commitments, though seemingly small, are the building blocks of a solid relationship with yourself. Whether it's committing to a daily walk, journaling your thoughts, or allowing yourself time to rest, each promise kept is a step towards self-assurance. When you honor these commitments, you reinforce the belief that you are worthy of care and attention. This practice of self-commitment nurtures an internal environment where trust and confidence thrive. Write down three small promises to yourself for the week and commit to them.

As you fulfill these promises, notice how each act strengthens your self-trust, transforming your internal dialogue from doubt to affirmation. The consistency in showing up for yourself fosters a profound sense of reliability and self-worth, encouraging a positive cycle of growth and empowerment.

Creating a safe space within yourself involves cultivating kindness, forgiveness, and encouragement. It's about building an internal sanctuary where you can retreat when the world feels overwhelming. This space becomes a refuge, a place where you can find solace and support. Practicing self-forgiveness is a vital part of this process. Acknowledge that mistakes are part of the human experience and remind yourself, "I'm learning, and I deserve grace."

This mantra helps dissolve the harshness of self-criticism, replacing it with understanding and acceptance. Consider the question, "What would your life look like if you treated yourself like your dearest friend?" Reflect on how you would support and encourage a beloved friend and extend that same compassion to yourself. This reflection invites you to nurture a relationship with yourself that is rich in empathy and kindness, providing a foundation for resilience and self-love.

As you build this relationship, you naturally enhance your ability to connect with others. Self-love becomes the lens through which you view the world. It influences how you interact, how you perceive challenges, and how you engage in relationships. This chapter serves as a reminder that embracing yourself fully is not just an act of self-care, but a pivotal step towards thriving in all areas of life.

With a solid foundation of self-love, you are better equipped to form meaningful connections, experience joy, and navigate challenges with grace. As we move forward, consider how this relationship with yourself can empower you to cultivate deeper and more authentic bonds with those around you.

9

10 Ways to Become the Most Popular Person in the Room

Have you ever walked into a room, feeling as though the air is thick with expectation, and wondered how some people seem to effortlessly attract attention and admiration? It often seems like a mysterious quality, something only a few possess. However, the secret lies not in some elusive charm but in the power of authenticity. Authenticity is a magnetic force, one that draws people in, creating connections that are both genuine and lasting. It is about embracing who you are, without the shroud of pretense. This chapter explores how being true to yourself can elevate your presence, making you not just popular, but genuinely cherished by those around you.

1. Be Real, People Love That

Authenticity is not just a trait; it is a way of living that instills trust and reinforces self-acceptance. When you present yourself authentically, you communicate a silent message of confidence and integrity. People connect with authenticity, not perfection. They are drawn to those who are unapologetically themselves, who embrace their quirks and imperfections.

By being genuine, you free yourself from the exhausting need to maintain a facade, allowing you to feel more comfortable in your skin. This comfort radiates outward, creating a welcoming aura that invites others to do the same. Imagine the relief of shedding the weight of perfectionism, of allowing your true self to shine. This act of self-liberation not only strengthens your self-esteem but also encourages those around you to embrace their authenticity.

Consider the story of David, a reserved young man who always felt the pressure to fit in. For years, he wore the mask of extroversion, attending gatherings and engaging in conversations that left him drained. One day, he decided to drop the mask. Instead of forcing himself into roles that didn't suit him, he embraced his introspective nature. He began sharing his love for niche hobbies, something he once hid. To his surprise, people responded with genuine interest.

They appreciated his honesty and found his passion infectious. By being true to himself, David not only felt more at ease but also forged deeper connections. His authenticity became a beacon, drawing others who appreciated him for who he truly was. This journey taught David that popularity doesn't come from blending in, but from standing out as your authentic self.

Reflection Section: Embrace Your True Self

Reflect on the aspects of yourself that you may have hidden or altered to fit in. What makes you unique? How can you embrace these traits in your daily interactions? Consider the following prompts to guide your reflection:

- **Identify a Quirk:** Write down a trait or interest that you've kept hidden. How might sharing this aspect of yourself create deeper connections?
- **Explore Authenticity:** Reflect on a recent interaction where you felt the need to conform. How did it feel? What might have changed if you had shown your true self?
- **Set an Intention:** Commit to embracing one authentic trait in your next social interaction. Notice how it feels and how others respond.

By engaging in self-reflection, you can better understand how authenticity shapes your interactions. Embracing your true self is a powerful step toward building genuine connections and becoming the person others naturally gravitate toward.

2. Make Others Feel Seen

Imagine a conversation where you feel genuinely heard, where every word you utter is met with attentive eyes and open ears. This is the power of giving someone your full attention. Practicing active listening is not just about hearing words; it's about truly understanding the speaker's message and emotions. When you listen without planning your next response, you engage more deeply, fostering empathy and building rapport.

This connection not only enriches your interactions but also enhances your emotional intelligence. By tuning into others, you appreciate the shared human experience, finding common ground and deepening your capacity for connection. Active listening transforms everyday conversations into meaningful exchanges, leaving both parties feeling valued and understood.

Consider the impact of asking questions that matter. Instead of the routine "How are you?" consider a more engaging approach, such as "What's something exciting happening in your life right now?" This shifts the focus from mundane pleasantries to topics that invite genuine dialogue. Meaningful questions encourage others to share their passions and interests, revealing layers of their personality and life experiences.

This not only makes the other person feel valued but also allows you to explore shared values and interests. As you navigate these conversations, you uncover commonalities that strengthen your bond, fostering mutual authenticity. By expressing curiosity, you create opportunities for deeper understanding and connection, enriching the tapestry of your social interactions.

3. Let Your Smile Do the Talking

"A warm smile can be a powerful tool", transcending language and cultural barriers to convey friendliness and approachability

(Hyper Blog, n.d.). It is a simple gesture, yet it can transform interactions, setting a positive tone from the outset. When you smile, you not only make others feel at ease, but you also trigger a cascade of positive emotions within yourself. This is because smiling activates neural circuits that enhance mood, reduce stress, and promote feelings of happiness.

It's not just for others; it's a way to cultivate your own optimism and inner peace. By practicing smiling more often, you can boost your self-confidence and make social situations more enjoyable. Imagine walking into a room with a smile as your calling card. It invites connection and signals openness. Your smile becomes a beacon, attracting those around you and creating an atmosphere of warmth and inclusivity.

Beyond the immediate impact of a smile, your body language speaks volumes before you utter a single word. It reflects your self-esteem and can shape how others perceive you. When you carry yourself with confidence, it projects self-assurance and invites respect. Simple adjustments in posture can make a significant difference. Stand tall, relax your shoulders, and maintain an open body posture. These subtle changes not only enhance your outward appearance but also reinforce an internal sense of self-assurance.

As you navigate social settings, consider how your physical presence communicates your readiness to engage, listen, and connect. Your energy speaks before you do, setting the stage for meaningful interactions. By consciously cultivating confident body language, you create an inviting space where others feel comfortable and valued. In this way, your smile and posture become integral parts of your communication, enhancing your ability to connect and be seen as approachable and genuine.

4. Lighten the Mood With Laughter

Imagine the tension easing from your shoulders as a genuine laugh escapes your lips. Learning to laugh at yourself is a powerful way to embrace your imperfections and practice self-acceptance. It's not about highlighting flaws but rather acknowledging them with a light heart. This form of humor, gentle and self-deprecating, allows you to show others that you're comfortable in your own skin.

When you share funny, relatable moments, you invite others to connect with you on a human level, breaking down barriers and fostering a sense of camaraderie. Humor becomes more than just a social tool; it becomes a means of releasing tension, allowing you to approach life's challenges with a sense of ease and self-compassion.

Fostering lightheartedness doesn't just enhance your interactions; it builds resilience. Humor has the unique ability to reframe challenges, transforming them into opportunities for growth. Consider a day when everything seemed to go wrong like the spilled coffee, the missed bus, the forgotten meeting. Instead of succumbing to frustration, imagine finding humor in the chaos. This shift in perspective can change not only your mood but also how you tackle problems.

By using humor to view obstacles through a different lens, you develop a mindset that sees possibilities instead of setbacks. This approach not only helps you but also encourages those around you to see problems in a new light. It creates an environment where laughter becomes a shared experience, strengthening bonds and promoting a positive outlook. Laughter, in its simplicity, can be a profound act of healing and connection reminding us all to take life a little less seriously.

5. Be the Kind of Person Who Lifts Others Up

Envision a world where every interaction leaves you feeling enriched, simply because someone took a moment to acknowledge your strengths. Celebrating others' successes is a powerful way to reflect your sense of abundance and security. When you genuinely compliment someone, it not only strengthens your bond but also builds your confidence as someone who uplifts others. Imagine the impact of telling a colleague, "Your presentation was inspiring," and watching their face light up.

This simple act reinforces your own positive qualities, cultivating a mindset of gratitude and fulfillment. In a world often focused on competition, choosing to celebrate others' achievements highlights your secure sense of self. It shows that you believe in the abundance of success and that there is enough room for everyone to shine. This attitude not only nurtures your relationships but also reflects a deep-seated confidence in yourself and your abilities.

Small gestures of kindness can profoundly nurture your authenticity and emotional depth. Remembering someone's name, for instance, or following up on a conversation shows that you care and are reliable. These acts may seem minor, yet they hold significant weight in building trust and rapport. Picture meeting someone new at a social event. Days later, you send a quick message asking about the hobby they mentioned.

This follow-up reinforces your connection and demonstrates reliability, enhancing your sense of self-worth as someone who values relationships. By making people feel important, you cultivate an atmosphere of mutual respect and appreciation. This not only strengthens your bonds with others but also deepens your understanding of yourself. Such gestures are reflections of your character, small yet powerful acts that reveal your commitment to building meaningful connections. They remind you that being attentive and present can transform relationships, creating a network of support and positivity around you.

6. Show Up for Others

Reliability is more than a trait; it's a testament to your integrity and self-discipline. When you commit to being dependable, you establish a foundation of trust, not just with others but within yourself. Imagine the strength of being someone others can rely on, someone whose word is as solid as stone. This consistency builds a sense of purpose and reinforces your confidence. Being dependable means showing up when you say you will, honoring commitments, and being present in moments that matter.

It's about creating a sense of security for those around you, knowing they can count on you in times of need. This reliability becomes a pillar of your character, one that others admire and respect. It is through these small, consistent actions that trust is cultivated and relationships are strengthened.

Helping others is a reflection of your values and an expression of compassion. When you choose to assist someone, even in seemingly insignificant ways, you align your actions with the principles you hold dear. This alignment reinforces your identity as a compassionate person, someone who contributes positively to the world around you. It's not about grand gestures but about the everyday opportunities to lend a hand, offer support, or simply be present.

These acts of kindness not only benefit those you help but also build your self-esteem. They remind you of your capacity for goodness and foster a sense of fulfillment. By being attentive to the needs of others, you cultivate a mindset of empathy and generosity, traits that enrich your own life as well as those you touch. In a world that moves at a relentless pace, taking a moment to help someone can create ripples of positivity that extend far beyond the initial act.

7. Make People Feel Comfortable Around You

In any social setting, the ability to adapt is a powerful tool that reflects both emotional intelligence and self-awareness. Reading the room involves tuning into the subtle cues and dynamics that define an environment. This awareness allows you to adjust your tone and energy, not as a means of changing who you are, but to show consideration for others' feelings.

Imagine being in a lively gathering and sensing a quieter, more reflective mood. By softening your approach, you demonstrate empathy and respect, which invites others to relax and engage more openly. Adaptability is not about losing yourself; rather, it's about showing that you're attuned to the social nuances that can make or break a connection.

Being approachable without being overbearing requires a delicate balance in social interactions. It's about creating a space where others feel comfortable and valued, without overwhelming them with your presence. This balance builds both confidence and mindfulness, fostering an environment where everyone feels at ease.

Picture yourself in a conversation, actively listening while maintaining a relaxed demeanor. This approach encourages others to share freely, knowing they have your genuine attention. By being present and mindful, you enhance your self-assurance, knowing that your presence contributes positively to the interaction.

This balance also nurtures your inner confidence, reinforcing the belief that you can navigate social settings with ease and authenticity. As you practice this awareness, you'll find that your ability to make others feel comfortable not only strengthens your connections but also enriches your sense of fulfillment.

8. Use Your Words to Build People Up

Words hold a transformative power that can elevate not only those around you but also yourself. When you choose to speak with kindness, you engage in a practice of gratitude that enriches your self-image and strengthens the bonds you share with others. Picture a moment when you sincerely tell a colleague, "I admire your hard work."

Such a statement does more than just acknowledge their efforts; it reinforces your habit of seeking and recognizing the good in others. This habit becomes a mirror, reflecting an image of yourself as someone who values and uplifts those around you. In a world often filled with criticism and judgment, choosing to speak kindly becomes a radical act of positivity and empowerment. This practice nurtures a sense of community, where everyone feels valued and motivated to contribute their best.

Conversely, avoiding gossip and negativity preserves your mental peace and aligns with your core values. It might be tempting to engage in gossip as a way to bond over shared opinions; however, this often leads to a spiral of negativity that can taint your well-being. Instead, focus on constructive conversations that build trust and reinforce your self-discipline. When you find yourself in conversations that veer toward negativity, guide them back to more positive topics.

This not only helps maintain your mental clarity but also sets a standard for those around you, encouraging a culture of respect and support. By consciously choosing positivity, you create an environment where open, honest, and uplifting dialogue thrives. This choice reflects your commitment to personal growth and the creation of meaningful, lasting relationships.

9. Be Curious, Not Judgmental

Imagine walking into a room full of diverse people, each with their own stories and experiences. Now, instead of forming quick judgments, what if you approached each person with genuine curiosity? This mindset shift can open doors to self-growth and broaden your horizons in ways you might not expect. Curiosity challenges assumptions and invites empathy, helping you see beyond surface impressions and understand the depth of another's journey.

When you ask about someone's passions, you not only learn something new but also connect on a deeper level. It's a simple yet profound way to bridge gaps and build meaningful relationships. This approach encourages open-mindedness, showing that everyone has something valuable to offer, including insights that can enrich your own life. By embracing curiosity, you create a space where learning and connection thrive, fostering an environment where differences are celebrated and shared understanding is cultivated.

Celebrating differences is not just about tolerance; it's about seeing the beauty in what makes each of us unique. When you take the time to appreciate others' uniqueness, you also begin to see the value in your individuality. This appreciation fosters self-acceptance, as you recognize that diversity enriches the human experience. By valuing differences, you challenge the notion that there's only one right way to be. Instead, you learn to treasure your quirks, realizing they contribute to the rich tapestry of life.

This mindset can transform your interactions, encouraging you to approach each person with an open heart and mind, ready to learn and grow. In doing so, you create a world where everyone feels valued and respected, fostering a community built on mutual appreciation and understanding. This way of engaging with others not only strengthens your relationships but also deepens your understanding of yourself, making you more resilient and empathetic in the process.

10. Leave Everyone Better Than You Found Them

In this fast-paced world, filled with fleeting interactions, there is profound power in leaving each person you meet a bit better than you found them. This isn't just about grand gestures but rather about the subtle, meaningful ways you can impact others. Reframing this concept as an opportunity for self-reflection invites you to consider how your presence influences those around you.

Maya Angelou beautifully encapsulated this idea: "People may forget what you said, but they'll never forget how you made them feel." By expressing gratitude or offering encouragement, you not only uplift those you interact with but also reinforce your own positive outlook.

Picture the warmth of a simple, heartfelt "thank you" or the lightness that follows a sincere compliment. These moments may seem small, but they create ripples that extend far beyond the initial encounter. They enhance your sense of fulfillment, reminding you of the power you hold to inspire and elevate others.

Spreading gratitude and positivity goes beyond enhancing personal connections. It fortifies your sense of joy. This practice is a conscious choice, a decision to focus on the abundance in life rather than its shortcomings. Consider ending every interaction by reflecting on one positive aspect, whether it's something you learned, a shared laugh, or an act of kindness.

This reflection leaves others feeling valued and acknowledged, fostering a mindset of abundance and gratitude within yourself. It's an approach that shifts your focus from scarcity to abundance, cultivating a joy that is both deep and lasting. By consciously choosing gratitude, you create an environment where positivity thrives, encouraging others to embrace the same outlook.

This mindset not only enriches your connections but also strengthens your emotional resilience, equipping you to face challenges with grace and optimism. Each positive interaction becomes a steppingstone, building a foundation of joy and fulfillment that supports you in all aspects of life.

As this chapter concludes, remember that the essence of becoming the most popular person in the room lies in authenticity, empathy, and positivity. These qualities create genuine connections, leaving a lasting impact on those you encounter. As you move forward, consider how these principles can shape your interactions, empowering you to foster deeper relationships and embrace the next chapter of self-discovery.

Now that you understand how to create meaningful connections, the next step is learning how to sustain them by fostering trust, emotional depth, and personal boundaries.

10

Courage: The Key to Building Deeper Relationships

Imagine standing on the edge of a vast ocean, the water stretching endlessly before you. The horizon is both daunting and exhilarating, teeming with possibilities yet unknown. To step into this ocean and to embrace the vastness of life is an act of courage. It is the willingness to venture into the depths of the unknown, to face the ebb and flow of life with open arms.

Courage in relationships is much like this ocean; it requires stepping beyond the familiar shores of comfort and predictability, into a realm where vulnerability and authenticity reign supreme. This chapter invites you to explore the transformative power of courage, urging you to show up and engage with life in ways that nurture your deepest connections.

The Courage to Show Up

In life, the biggest shifts often begin with a single step. But taking that step whether it's introducing yourself to someone new, pursuing an opportunity, or speaking up when it matters requires courage. The fear of rejection, failure, or looking foolish can be paralyzing, keeping you stuck in the background rather than fully engaging with the world around you. But showing up isn't about being fearless; it's about taking action despite your fears. It's about recognizing that the only way to grow, connect, and truly live is to participate.

Think about the last time you hesitated because you were afraid of the outcome. Maybe you avoided a conversation, held back from sharing an idea, or convinced yourself that you weren't good enough. These small moments accumulate, reinforcing patterns of avoidance and self-doubt. The more you stay on the sidelines, the more comfortable it becomes to remain there. But every time you choose to show up, you rewrite the script. You prove to yourself that discomfort isn't a stop sign. It's a signal that you're stretching beyond your comfort zone.

Consider the story of Michael, a man who spent years avoiding situations that required him to put himself out there. He convinced himself that people weren't interested in what he had to say, so he remained quiet in social settings and professional meetings. But when he finally pushed himself to join a book club, something shifted. The first meeting was intimidating, but he showed up anyway.

The second meeting felt a little easier, and by the third, he was contributing to discussions with confidence. Michael didn't change overnight, but his willingness to step forward, even when it felt uncomfortable, set off a chain reaction in his life. He built friendships, strengthened his confidence, and discovered that the world wasn't nearly as intimidating as he once believed.

The Domino Effect of Showing Up

What makes showing up so powerful is that it builds momentum. The first time you take a risk, it might feel overwhelming. But the next time, it's slightly easier. And the time after that? Even easier. This is the domino effect of courage: one small action leads to another, gradually transforming the way you engage with the world.

When you start putting yourself in situations that stretch you, something incredible happens. You stop letting fear dictate your choices. You realize that most of the things you once dreaded weren't nearly as catastrophic as you imagined. Maybe that awkward conversation didn't ruin a friendship. Maybe that professional risk led to an unexpected opportunity. The more you practice showing up, the more you prove to yourself that you are capable of handling whatever comes next.

Practical Action: Take One Intentional Step

Fear often thrives in uncertainty. The best way to weaken its hold is through action. This week, challenge yourself to do one thing that pushes you beyond your comfort zone. It doesn't have to be monumental. It just has to be intentional.

- Start a conversation with someone new instead of waiting for them to speak first.
- Raise your hand in a meeting or share an idea you've been holding back.
- Reach out to an old friend you've lost touch with.
- Take a risk. Apply for the job, sign up for the class, and step onto the stage.

Write down your commitment and the specific action you'll take. Once you've done it, reflect on the experience. How did it feel? What did you learn? Even if the outcome wasn't perfect, you'll have taken an important step in shifting your mindset from avoidance to engagement.

Showing up isn't about instant transformation. It's about training yourself to stop waiting for the "perfect moment" and start embracing the opportunities in front of you. Each time you push past your hesitation, you gain confidence in your ability to navigate the unknown.

And when you make showing up a habit, you don't just change your own life, you inspire others to do the same. Courage is contagious. The more you step forward; the more permission you give to those around you to step forward too. You never know who might be watching and finding the courage to show up because you did.

The Courage to Be Seen for Who You Are

Imagine a life where every interaction is an opportunity to reveal, not conceal, your true self. Yet, for many, the fear of judgment makes this vulnerability feel like too great a risk. It's easier to blend in, say what's expected, and hide behind a carefully crafted image. But in doing so, we deny ourselves the deeper, more meaningful relationships that only come when we allow others to see us as we truly are.

Why We Hide And Why It's Time to Stop

From an early age, many of us learn to filter ourselves based on how we think others will perceive us. Maybe you were told you were too sensitive, too quiet, too loud, or not enough of something. Over time, these messages shape the way we present ourselves. We learn to mask the parts of us that might not be universally accepted, believing that if we show up as we are, we might not belong.

But the irony is this: The very things we try to hide are often what make us most relatable. The quirks, the struggles, the imperfect edges, these are what draw people in and not push them away. Consider Emily, who always wore a mask of confidence and perfection. She believed that revealing her struggles would make her seem weak. However, when she finally confided in a close friend about her fears and insecurities, she was met with understanding and support. That moment of honesty deepened their friendship in a way surface-level interactions never could. By allowing herself to be seen, she permitted others to do the same.

When you hide parts of yourself, you might think you're protecting yourself from rejection. But what you're doing is limiting the depth of connection available to you. No one can truly know you if you're always editing yourself to fit an imagined ideal.

The Power of Letting Yourself Be Seen

So, what does it mean to have the courage to be seen? It means showing up in the world without waiting for permission. It means expressing your opinions, even if they aren't the most popular. It means allowing yourself to be wrong, imperfect, and still learning. It's knowing that true confidence doesn't come from external approval but from internal acceptance.

It also means embracing vulnerability not as a weakness, but as a gateway to connection. Brené Brown, a renowned researcher on vulnerability and courage, captures this perfectly:

"Courage starts with showing up and letting ourselves be seen."

If you've ever hesitated before sharing something personal, fearing how it might be received, you've felt this tension. "The fear of being judged, misunderstood, or dismissed" can be overwhelming (Magnetic Media, 2023).

But here's the truth: The relationships that matter, the ones worth investing in aren't built on facades. They're built on honesty. On showing up as you are, even when it feels risky.

Practical Action: One Step Toward Authenticity

If being seen feels overwhelming, start small. Choose one aspect of yourself that you've been holding back whether it's a passion, an opinion, or a personal truth and find a way to express it.

- Share something personal with someone you trust.
- Let go of the need to edit yourself in casual interactions.

Pay attention to what happens when you do. Does the world fall apart? Or do you find that people respect you more for being real? Often, the fear of being seen is far greater than the reality of it.

Letting yourself be loved and accepted requires the courage to open up, to allow others into the sacred spaces of your heart. It's about dismantling the barriers that keep people at a distance and embracing the connections that bring joy and fulfillment. When you invite others to see the real you, you create bonds that heal, strengthen, and deepen relationships. This openness transforms interactions from superficial exchanges to meaningful connections that enrich your life.

As you embrace this journey of authenticity, remember that it is not about perfection but about embracing your humanity. It's about recognizing that your imperfections are not flaws to be hidden but unique aspects to be celebrated. By allowing yourself to be seen, you create a ripple effect of courage and authenticity, inspiring others to do the same. This shared vulnerability fosters a community of support and understanding, where each person is valued for who they truly are.

The Courage to Keep Growing Together

Imagine a garden where each plant, though unique in its needs and growth patterns, thrives beside others in harmony. Relationships, much like this garden, require attention, patience, and the willingness to accommodate change. Yet, change whether in relationships or within us can feel unsettling. It challenges the comfort of the familiar, asking us to grow beyond what we once were. But if there's one thing we've learned throughout this book, it's that growth is always worth the discomfort.

In relationships, change is often the key to deeper connection. When you embrace growth instead of resisting it, you allow yourself and those around you to evolve together. This requires courage. A willingness to show up even when things are uncertain, to listen when conversations get difficult, and to remain present even when change feels uncomfortable. True connection isn't about staying the same. It's about learning, adapting, and choosing to grow alongside the people who matter to you.

When Life Shifts, So Can We

This process of growing together doesn't happen in grand, dramatic moments. It happens in the small, everyday choices we make to invest in our relationships. It's when a friend opens up about a personal struggle, and instead of brushing it off, you sit with them in their discomfort. It's when a relationship changes, and rather than resisting that change, you ask, "How can we navigate this together?" It's when life pulls you in different directions, but you still make the effort to check in, to listen, and to show up even when it would be easier to withdraw.

In friendships, growth might mean learning to communicate differently, especially when life circumstances shift. Maybe one of you moves away, starts a new career, or enters a new stage of life. Instead of assuming the friendship will naturally sustain itself, you take intentional steps whether through deeper conversations, mutual check-ins, or new ways of spending time together.

In romantic relationships, growth might mean letting go of the idea that love should always feel effortless. Love isn't just about the highs, it's about choosing each other during the hard times, too. It's about recognizing that people evolve, and that long-term connection requires continual learning, adaptation, and effort. It's about asking, "How can we grow through this instead of apart from each other?"

In family relationships, growth often requires forgiveness and understanding. It might mean seeing a parent or sibling not just for who they were in the past, but for who they are now. It might mean setting healthier boundaries, having difficult conversations, or simply accepting that some relationships will never look exactly the way we imagined but they can still be meaningful in their own way.

Growing together doesn't mean avoiding conflict or pretending things never change. It means being brave enough to face challenges head-on and trust that the relationships worth keeping will weather the storms and come out stronger on the other side.

Commitment to Your Own Growth

To cultivate this mindset of growth, consider how you engage with the people in your life. Do you create space for honest conversations? Do you invite feedback, even when it's hard to hear? Do you recognize when someone you care about is changing and support their evolution instead of clinging to who they used to be? Asking yourself these questions regularly ensures that you are not only growing as an individual but also fostering relationships that can withstand life's inevitable shifts.

But this idea of continuous growth isn't just about relationships. It's also about how you keep showing up for yourself. It's about recognizing that self-improvement doesn't end when you reach a milestone. It's about continuing to challenge yourself, to push past fear, and to embrace the unknown with curiosity rather than hesitation. The courage to grow together isn't just about maintaining strong relationships with others. It's about maintaining a strong relationship with yourself, trusting that you are capable of becoming the person you want to be.

As you close this chapter and prepare to take what you've learned into the real world, remind yourself that this is just the beginning. Personal growth is a lifelong journey, and every moment presents an opportunity to lean into courage rather than fear. The people in your life, the ones who truly matter are worth the effort, just as you are.

Now, it's time to take everything you've learned and put it into action.

Conclusion:

You Are the Author of Your Story

As we come to the final pages of this book, take a moment to reflect on how far you've come. Maybe you started this journey feeling stuck in cycles of self-doubt, replaying old fears, or questioning your place in the world. Maybe you've spent years wrestling with relationships feeling misunderstood, unseen, or unsure of how to form meaningful connections. Wherever you were when you first picked up this book, I want you to recognize something powerful. You are not the same person who began this journey.

Through each chapter, you've challenged yourself to question old beliefs, recognize toxic patterns, and step into the discomfort of growth. That takes courage. It's easy to stay stuck. It's easy to keep telling ourselves the same limiting stories, avoiding change because it feels safer than the unknown. But you chose something different. You chose to lean in, to rethink the way you see yourself and others, and to take real, actionable steps toward the life you truly want.

And that's something to be proud of.

This Is Just the Beginning

Growth isn't a one-time event; it's a lifelong commitment. You've laid the foundation, but your journey doesn't end here. The truths you've discovered in this book are meant to be lived, practiced, and revisited over and over again. Because here's the reality:

- There will be days when your inner critic creeps back in. But now, you know it's lying to you. You have the tools to challenge those thoughts and rewrite your narrative.
- There will be moments when you feel insecure in social situations. But now, you understand that confidence isn't about perfection, it's about showing up, embracing who you are, and focusing on how you make others feel.
- There will be relationships that challenge you. But now, you recognize the difference between connection and control, between trust and toxicity. You know what it means to invest in real, meaningful friendships.
- There will be setbacks. But now, you understand that growth isn't about avoiding failure, it's about learning from it, choosing to keep going, and refusing to let fear define you.

This is your story to write and you hold the pen.

Keep Going, Even When It's Hard

If there's one message, I want you to take away from this book, it's this: You are capable of change. You are worthy of connection. You are enough.

The biggest lie we tell ourselves is that we have to be someone else to be loved, to belong, or to feel confident. That's not true. The relationships that matter, the moments that define us, the confidence that lasts, it all comes from one simple truth: Being unapologetically yourself.

So, keep growing. Keep pushing forward. Keep rewriting the narratives that no longer serve you. You don't have to be fearless. You just have to be brave enough to try.

Thank You for Letting Me Be Part of Your Journey

Writing this book has been a deeply personal journey for me, because I know what it's like to struggle with these things. I know what it's like to feel like you're always one step behind, always doubting yourself, always wondering if you're truly good enough. And if this book has given you even one moment of clarity, one shift in perspective, or one tool to help you feel more confident, then it was worth writing.

No book, no mentor, and no single moment will ever complete you. Growth is a daily decision, and the person you're becoming is shaped by the choices you make moving forward.

I believe in you. I believe in your ability to grow, to connect, and to create a life filled with meaning and authentic relationships. And I hope that, as you close this book, you believe in yourself too.

With gratitude,

Robert Hayes

References

- Self-Compassion Research by Kristin Neff https://self-compassion.org/the-research/
- Research https://brenebrown.com/the-research/
- Cognitive behavior therapy (CBT) https://www.betterhealth.vic.gov.au/health/conditionsandtreatments/cognitive-behaviour-therapy
- The Cost and Benefits of Emotional Honesty https://www.psychologytoday.com/us/blog/stronger-the-broken-places/201112/the-cost-and-benefits-emotional-honesty
- How Negativity Can Ruin Relationships - Psychology Today https://www.psychologytoday.com/us/blog/couples-thrive/202002/how-negativity-can-ruin-relationships
- Self-Centeredness - Dr. Michael McGee https://drmichaelmcgee.com/self-centeredness/#:~:text=Being%20self%2Dcentered%20is%20costly,You%20cannot%20be%20empathic.
- Trust issues: Signs, causes, and how to overcome them https://thriveworks.com/help-with/relationships/trust-issues/
- Gossip Can Destroy Friendships And Careers https://timesuniononline.com/news/2021/sep/06/gossip-can-destroy-friendships-and-careers/

- Our deepest fear is not that we are inadequate.... https://www.goodreads.com/quotes/928-our-deepest-fear-is-not-that-we-are-inadequate-our
- Self-Compassion by Kristin Neff: Join the Community Now https://self-compassion.org/
- Oscar Wilde on Selfishness, Unselfishness, and Conformity https://jjmilt.substack.com/p/oscar-wilde-on-selfishness-unselfishness
- Quote by Mohsin Hamid: "Empathy is about finding echoes ... https://www.goodreads.com/quotes/9076745-empathy-is-about-finding-echoes-of-another-person-in-yourself
- Quote by Brené Brown: "Self-Compassion https://www.goodreads.com/quotes/1178626-self-compassion-stop-beating-yourself-up-and-leave-insecurity-behind-she
- Treatment Approaches | Bauer Psychology https://www.bauerpsychology.com/treatment-approaches
- 8 Powerful Self-Compassion Exercises & Worksheets ... https://positivepsychology.com/self-compassion-exercises-worksheets/
- Carol Dweck: A Summary of Growth and Fixed Mindsets https://fs.blog/carol-dweck-mindset/
- Self-Centeredness - Dr. Michael McGee https://drmichaelmcgee.com/self-centeredness/#:~:text=Self%2Dcenteredness%20damages%20relationships%2C%20because,centered%20

ruminations%20causes%20more%20anxiety.

- Understanding Others: The Importance of Perspective Taking https://everydayspeech.com/sel-implementation/understanding-others-the-importance-of-perspective-taking/
- How Gratitude Helps Your Friendships Grow https://greatergood.berkeley.edu/article/item/how_gratitude_helps_your_friendships_grow#:~:text=Research%20suggests%20that%20gratitude%20plays,role%20in%20building%20a%20relationship. &text=A%20great%20deal%20of%20research,maintain%2C%20and%20strengthen%20our%20relationships.
- How Mindfulness Helps Us to Build Meaningful Social ... https://www.mindandlife.org/media/how-mindfulness-helps-us-to-build-meaningful-social-connections/
- Crafting a Personal Narrative Identity: Embracing Change https://psychologyfanatic.com/narrative-identity/
- Elizabeth Loftus https://en.wikipedia.org/wiki/Elizabeth Loftus
- How a CBT Therapist Can Help You Overcome Limiting Beliefs https://bayareacbtcenter.com/how-a-cbt-therapist-in-san-francisco-can-help-you-overcome-limiting-beliefs/#:~:text=For%20instance%2C%20CBT%20therapists%20teach,identifying%20and%20challenging%20irrational%20beliefs.
- Benefits of Vision Boards for Personal Growth https://

californiaprimerecovery.com/benefits-of-vision-boards-for-personal-growth/

- Cognitive Distortions and Self-Esteem https://www.gatewaytosolutions.org/cognitive-distortions-and-self-esteem/
- CBT Techniques: 25 Cognitive Behavioral Therapy ... https://positivepsychology.com/cbt-cognitive-behavioral-therapy-techniques-worksheets/
- Positive Reinforcement in Psychology (Definition + ... https://positivepsychology.com/positive-reinforcement-psychology/
- How To Rewrite Your Own Story – Lessons From Narrative ... https://ctrinstitute.com/blog/how-to-rewrite-your-own-story-lessons-from-narrative-therapy/
- How To Safely Embrace Your Flaws and Imperfections | WTG https://williamsburgtherapygroup.com/blog/how-to-safely-embrace-your-flaws-and-imperfections
- 80 Self-Confidence Positive Affirmations for Self-Esteem \u0026 ... https://www.betterup.com/blog/affirmations-for-confidence
- The importance of self-care for maintaining mental health https://today.marquette.edu/2024/08/the-importance-of-self-care-for-maintaining-mental-health/
- Silencing Your Inner Critic https://www.psychologytoday.com/us/articles/201903/silencing-your-inner-critic

- The Importance of Authenticity | Berkeley Exec Ed https://executive.berkeley.edu/thought-leadership/blog/importance-authenticity
- Active Listening: A Key Element in Building Strong ... https://everydayspeech.com/blog-posts/general/active-listening-a-key-element-in-building-strong-relationships/
- 12 Ways to Have More Confident Body Language https://www.verywellmind.com/ten-ways-to-have-more-confident-body-language-3024855
- Humor in Interpersonal Communication https://oxfordre.com/communication/display/10.1093/acrefore/9780190228613.001.0001/acrefore-9780190228613-e-660?d=%2F10.1093%2Facrefore%2F9780190228613.001.0001%2Facrefore-9780190228613-e-660&p=emailA6tJHCipY9F4.
- The 45 Best Brené Brown Quotes About Courage, Shame ... https://fourminutebooks.com/brene-brown-quotes/#:~:text=%E2%80%9CVulnerability%20is%20not%20winning%20or,our%20greatest%20measure%20of%20courage.%E2%80%9D
- Building Authentic Connections: Embracing Vulnerability https://www.psychologytoday.com/us/blog/on-second-thought/202312/building-authentic-connections-embracing-vulnerability
- Powerful personal stories of courage https://www.goodsams.org.au/article/powerful-personal-stories-of-

courage/

- Strategies For Fostering Growth In A Relationship https://www.betterhelp.com/advice/relations/fostering-growth-in-a-relationship-key-strategies-for-success/
- GuidanceTT. 72% of people cite selfishness as one of the most intolerable traits in relationships https://www.guidancett.com/selfishness-relationships
- PsychCentral. The scarcity mindset and its impact on relationships https://psychcentral.com/scarcity-mindset-relationships
- Why It Pays to Get Inside the Head of Your Opponent: The Differential Effects of Perspective Taking and Empathy in Negotiations https://doi.org/10.1037/a0017229
- Social Anxiety's Impact on Affective and Interpersonal Responses to Daily Social Interaction https://doi.org/10.1037/0022-3514.87.4.611
- The Social Effects of Reflecting on How One's Actions Impact Others https://journals.sagepub.com/doi/10.1177/0265407517702011
- Reciprocal Interactions and Life Satisfaction: The Impact of Meaningful Conversations https://guilfordjournals.com/doi/abs/10.1521/jscp.2013.32.1.23
- The Role of Generosity and Selflessness in Strengthening Relationships https://greatergood.berkeley.edu/article/item/the_science_of_generosity

- Setting New Year's Resolutions with Grace: The Etiquette of Personal Growth. https://www.poisedproper.com/post/setting-new-year-s-resolutions-with-grace-the-etiquette-of-personal-growth
- 20 best books on self acceptance - 2023 reading list & recommendations. https://paulfinchauthor.com/20-best-books-on-self-acceptance-2023-reading-list-recommendations/
- The Power Of Self-Compassion: Nurturing Your Mental Health And Wellbeing. https://www.serenitiespath.co.uk/post/the-power-of-self-compassion-nurturing-your-mental-health-and-wellbeing
- Middle Road: Finding Balance and Fulfillment in Life | Inoa Juice. https://inoajuice.com/middle-road-finding-balance-and-fulfillment-in-life/
- How Alcohol Destroys Your Relationships | Sanctuary Foundation. https://sanctuary-recovery.com/blog/how-alcohol-destroys-your-relationships/
- Cognitive-Behavioral Approaches To Stress. https://spinal-injury.net/cognitive-behavioral-approaches-to-stress/
- Leading Change - ADAPTABILITY is Better - RapidKnowHow. https://www.rapidknowhow.com/how-to-improve-your-adaptability-skills-in-2024/
- OnStoic. https://onstoic.com/tag/impact/

- The Importance of Soft Skills in Business Loan Brokering. https://www.brokersolutions.org/blog/soft-skills-in-business-loan-brokering
- What I Wish I Knew About Rights • blackspringpress.co.uk. https://blackspringpress.co.uk/what-i-wish-i-knew-about-rights/
- 12 Worst Responses to 'I'm Sorry'. https://parentportfolio.com/worst-responses-to-im-sorry/
- The Power of Thought: How Your Mind Shapes Your Reality - Live Life Magically!. https://livelifemagically.com/the-power-of-thought-how-your-mind-shapes-your-reality/
- Calm Is A Super Power â˜... Inspiration Power Boost. https://inspirationpowerboost.com/calm-is-a-super-power/
- Arcana: Unlocking our Subconscious with The Matrix of Destiny | The Matrix of Destiny. https://www.thematrixofdestiny.com/arcana-and-the-destiny-matrix-chart
- Why Consistently Performing Healthy Habits Is Vital for a Healthy Life. https://www.fly-bodies.com/post/the-power-of-consistency-key-to-health-and-fitness-success
- The Anatomy of Anxiety: Understanding Its Effects - Norman Hinks NLP & Hypnotherapy. https://normanhinks.com/index.php/my-blog/the-anatomy-of-anxiety-understanding-its-effects-and-nlp-based-

coping-mechanisms.html

- The Rules of Love: Mastering the Art of Meaningful Connections - خالصة كتاب. https://khkitab.com/the-rules-of-love/
- Embracing the Wisdom of the Three Gunas: 14th Chapter of the Gita. https://www.anaadi.org/post/embracing-the-wisdom-of-the-three-gunas-14th-chapter-of-the-gita
- 10 Transformative Habits to Kickstart Your Growth Journey this Spring - Nicole Commissiong. https://nicolecommissiong.com/2024/04/10-transformative-habits-to-kickstart-your-growth-journey-this-spring/
- How Can a Brighter Smile Boost Your Career Prospects? | Hyper Blog. http://hypermusic.ca/how-can-a-brighter-smile-boost-your-career-prospects/
- Acting Premier at Mental Health Panel Discussion – Magnetic Media. https://magneticmediatv.com/2023/05/acting-premier-at-mental-health-panel-discussion/

Get 3 FREE Tools That Change Everything

I appreciate you!!!

Thank you for reading Everyone Loves Me. These three free companion tools are deeply personal, born from my own healing, research, and hard-won lessons. They're the most powerful, practical resources I've ever created. If the book spoke to you, these will take you even deeper.

Click the link or scan the QR code below. Then just enter your email. I'll send you immediate access to all three free programs, along with additional resources as I continue to write and research solutions for you.

Three Free Tools. One New You

Drop the Mask. Be Seen. Be Loved. What kind of thinker are you? Take the quiz. Meet your mind. Then start thinking like someone who trusts themselves and lives without second-guessing every move.

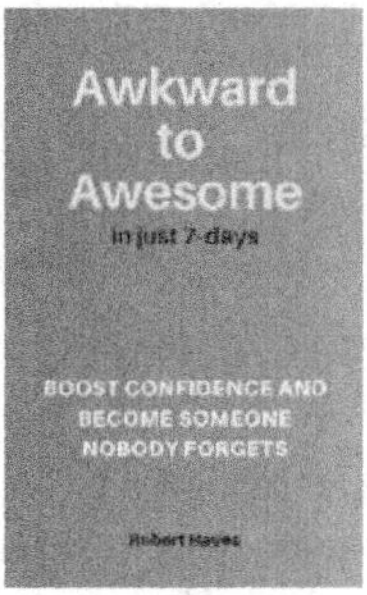

Boost Confidence and Become Someone Nobody Forgets.
Confidence isn't a mystery, it's a habit. Build it one small step at a time. From overthinking and awkward to unforgettable and magnetic in just one powerful week.

What Every Couple Needs But Nobody Teaches.
The repair manual you never got. Fix what's fading. Rebuild what matters. Real tools to reconnect deeply, before "fine" quietly turns into falling apart.

Don't Stop Here, Let's Go Deeper

Click the Link or Scan the QR Code for FREE Access

Visit: www.roberthayesbooks.com/loves/

A Personal Favor from Robert Hayes

I need your help...

If Everyone Loves Me meant something to you, if it helped you feel seen, stronger, or a little more loved, I'd be deeply grateful if you'd take 60 seconds to leave a great review on Amazon.

This book is my life's mission. Your review isn't just feedback, it's a lifeline.

Your words can encourage someone else to begin their healing, to feel hope, to believe change is possible.

This message spreads to one person at a time, not through ads, but through readers like you.

Thank you for reading. Thank you for being part of this.

Scan this QR Code to Leave a Review

Also, if you'd like to stay in the loop about upcoming books and updates, follow me on Instagram at **@robert_h_author**

or scan the QR Code:

@ROBERT_H_AUTHOR_

A Video That Might Change Your Life

Reading Everyone Loves Me is a powerful awakening.

But what if you could put it into action, faster, clearer, with more impact?

This short video is the Quick Start many of my most successful clients have used to transform everything.

It's not for everyone. But if you're serious about change, and want momentum, not just insight, this is where things really start moving.

No pressure. No expectations. Just one video that might flip the switch.

Watch now. The next version of you is waiting.

Visit: www.roberthayesbooks.com/loves/video

Or scan the QR Code below.

Printed in Dunstable, United Kingdom

76747955R00087